Kabbalah Revealed

Rav Michael Laitman, PhD
Introduction by: Professor Ervin Laszlo

Kabbalah Revealed

A Guide
to a More Peaceful Life

LAITMAN
KABBALAH PUBLISHERS

Rav Michael Laitman, PhD
Introduction by: Professor Ervin Laszlo

KABBALAH REVEALED
A Guide to a More Peaceful Life

Library of Congress Cataloging-in-Publication Data
Laitman, Michael.
Kabbalah revealed:
a guide to a more peaceful life /
Michael Laitman
p. cm.
ISBN 0-9781590-0-4
1. Cabalah. 2. Mysticism—Judaism.
3. Spiritual life—Judaism. I. Title.
BM525.L253 2006
296.1'6—dc22   2006031322

Copy Editor: Claire Gerus
Layout and Drawings: Baruch Khovov
Cover Design: Richard Aquan
Printing and Post Production: Uri Laitman
Executive Editor: Chaim Ratz

Cover photo: Manuscripts of Kabbalist Yehuda Ashlag,
courtesy of Bnei Baruch archives and Studio Yaniv, Israel.

FIRST EDITION: JANUARY 2007

Second printing 2009

KABBALAH REVEALED

TABLE OF CONTENTS

Biographies 9
Introduction 13

CHAPTER 1 - KABBALAH: THEN AND NOW 19
THE MASTER PLAN 19
THE CRADLE OF SCIENCE 21
    Other Routes 23
    The Big Questions 24
KABBALAH STEPS IN 24
    The Engine of Change 25
    Taking the Driver's Seat 26
HIDING, SEEKING, BUT NOT FINDING 28
    The Global Crisis Has a Happy End 30
    Egoism Is a Catch-22 30
THE NECESSITY OF ALTRUISM 32
    Enhanced Perception 34
    The Time Is Now 36
IN A NUTSHELL 37

CHAPTER 2 - THE GREATEST WISH OF ALL 39
SPRINGBOARD FOR GROWTH 40
    Behind Closed Doors 41
    The Evolution of Desires 43
HANDLING DESIRES 46
    A New Desire in Town 47
    A New Method for a New Desire 48
    Tikkun—the Correction of the Will to Receive 50
IN A NUTSHELL 52

CHAPTER 3 - THE ORIGIN OF CREATION 53
THE SPIRITUAL WORLDS 54
    Four Basic Phases 55
THE QUEST FOR THE THOUGHT OF CREATION 61
THE ROUTE 66
ADAM HA RISHON—THE COMMON SOUL 71
IN A NUTSHELL 73

CHAPTER 4 - OUR UNIVERSE 75
   THE PYRAMID 76
      As Above, So Below... 78
   UP THE LADDER 79
   THE DESIRE FOR SPIRITUALITY 84
   IN A NUTSHELL.. 90

CHAPTER 5 - WHOSE REALITY IS REALITY? 93
   THREE BOUNDARIES IN LEARNING KABBALAH 96
      First Boundary—What We Perceive..................................... 96
      Second Boundary—Where We Perceive 96
      Third Boundary—Who Perceives 97
   PERCEPTION OF REALITY 100
      A Nonexistent Reality 103
      The Measurement Mechanism.. 105
      The Sixth Sense... 106
      Where There's a Way, There Was a Will............................. 109
      The Thought of Creation.. 111
      Reshimot—Back to the Future 113
   IN A NUTSHELL.. 116

CHAPTER 6 - THE (NARROW) ROAD TO FREEDOM 119
   THE DARK BEFORE THE DAWN 121
      A Brave New World in Four Steps 126
   KNOW YOUR LIMITS... 129
      The Reins of Life 131
      Changing Society to Change Myself 133
   FOUR FACTORS... 135
   CHOOSING THE RIGHT ENVIRONMENT FOR CORRECTION 138
      No Anarchists 142
   THE EGO'S INEVITABLE DEATH 143
      The Cure 145
      Fake Freedom 147
      Conditions for Free Choice 149
   IMPLEMENTING FREE CHOICE.. 150
      Faith.. 150
      Reason 151
   IN A NUTSHELL.. 153

FURTHER READING...157

Biographies

RAV MICHAEL LAITMAN, PHD

Rav Michael Laitman, PhD, is an international authority on authentic Kabbalah. His background is highly unusual for one renowned in the spiritual: he was educated in the sciences, holds an MS in bio-cybernetics, and has pursued a successful scientific career, later turning to Kabbalah to further his scientific research. He received his PhD in Philosophy and Kabbalah from the Moscow Institute of Philosophy at the Russian Academy of Sciences.

In 1976, he began studying Kabbalah, and has been researching it ever since. In 1979, seeking new avenues in Kabbalah, he came across Kabbalist Rabbi Baruch Shalom HaLevi Ashlag (1906-1991), the firstborn son, and successor of Kabbalist Rabbi Yehuda Leib HaLevi Ashlag (1884-1954), known as Baal HaSulam for his

Sulam (Ladder) commentary on *The Book of Zohar*. Michael Laitman was so impressed with Baal HaSulam's son, that he became Baruch Ashlag's closest disciple and personal assistant, spending the bulk of his time in the company of his revered mentor, and absorbing as much as he could of his teachings.

Today, he is regarded as the foremost authority on Kabbalah, having authored thirty books on the subject, translated into ten languages. His live lessons are broadcast daily on cable TV and internet around the world. In recent years, he has become a sought-after lecturer in academic circles in the United States and Europe.

Dr. Laitman is the founder and president of Bnei Baruch - Kabbalah Education and Research Institute, which operates the largest and most extensive internet site on the subject of Kabbalah, *www.kabbalah.info*. The website provides unlimited access to Kabbalistic texts and media in over twenty languages, with 1.4 million hits per month. Since the year 2000, the *Encyclopedia Britannica* recognizes *kabbalah.info* as one of the largest internet sites for both number of visitors and quantity of educational and informational materials on the science of Kabbalah.

PROFESSOR ERVIN LASZLO

Prof. Ervin Laszlo, who graciously wrote the introduction to this book, is the founder and foremost exponent of Systems Philosophy and General Evolution Theory. Born in Budapest, Hungary in 1932, Laszlo made his debut as a concert pianist at the age of fifteen in New York, an event reported in *Life, Time, Newsweek*, and the international media.

Prof. Laszlo turned to science and philosophy in his mid-twenties and began publishing books and articles in 1963. In 1970 he received the State Doctorate, the highest degree of the Sorbonne, the University of Paris. In subsequent years he was awarded honorary PhDs in the United States, Canada, Finland, Russia, and Hungary.

In recognition of his commitment to global understanding and development, he received the 2001 Goi Award, the Peace Prize of Japan. He has written seventy-two books, translated into as many as eighteen languages.

INTRODUCTION

I am delighted and honored to have been asked to write the introduction to Dr. Laitman's *Kabbalah Revealed: A Guide to a More Peaceful Life*. Not only is the author a dear personal friend, he is, in my view, the foremost Kabbalist alive today, a genuine representative of a wisdom that has been kept secret for two millennia. Now that the wisdom of Kabbalah, among other indigenous wisdoms, is emerging full scale, I believe no other person is better suited to expound on its essence.

In today's world, the emergence of Kabbalah as an authentic means of instruction is of unique significance. It can help us regain awareness of the wisdom that our forefathers possessed, and which we have forgotten.

Indigenous wisdoms are appearing today precisely because our customary, mechanical school of thought has failed to provide the well-being and sustainability it had promised. A Chinese proverb warns, "If we do not change direction, we are likely to end up exactly where we are headed." When applied to contemporary humanity, this could prove disastrous:

Climate change is threatening to turn vast areas of our planet into unlivable, lifeless soil, unsuitable for human habitation and inadequate for food production.

Additionally, most of the world's economies have become less self-sufficient. This is ominously coupled with the worldwide diminution of food reserves. There is less available freshwater for well over half of the world's population. On average, more than 6,000 children perish each day from diarrhea caused by polluted water.

In many parts of the world, violence and terrorism have become the favored means to resolve conflicts. Hence, there is deepening insecurity in both rich and poor countries. Islamic fundamentalism is spreading throughout the Muslim world, neo-Nazi and other extremist movements are sprouting in Europe, and religious fanaticism is appearing the world over.

Thus, our very tenure on this planet is in question.

However, global breakdown is not mandatory. We can turn the tide, and the following scenario, too, is entirely possible:

As the latter part of this book will show, we can pull together and pursue shared objectives of peace and sustainability. Business leaders can recognize the groundswell of change and respond with goods and services that meet the shift in demand.

Global news and entertainment media might explore fresh perspectives and emerging social and cultural innovations, and a new vision of self and nature will emerge on the internet, on television, and in communication networks of enterprises and communities.

In civil society, a culture of alternative living and responsible values will lend support to policies of social and ecological sustainability. Measures will be taken to protect the environment, create effective food and resource distribution systems, develop and use sustainable energy, transport, and agricultural technologies.

In this positive outlook, funds will be redirected from the military and defense establishments to serve the needs of the people. Supported by these developments, national, international, and intercultural mistrust, ethnic and racial conflicts, oppression, economic inequity, and gender inequality will all give way to mutual trust and respect. People and communities will readily cooperate and form productive partnerships.

Thus, rather than breaking *down* in conflict and war, humanity will break *through*—not merely to a sustainable world of self-reliant and cooperating communities, but to a joyous future of peace, tranquility and complete self-fulfillment.

A peaceful and sustainable world can await us all, but alas, we are not presently headed in this direction. Einstein told us, "The significant problems we face cannot be solved at the same level of thinking at which we created them." Yet, we are trying to do just that. We are trying to fight terrorism, poverty, crime, environmental degradation, disease, and other "sicknesses of civilization" with the same methods that produced them in the first place. We are attempting technological fixes and temporary remedial measures. Yet we have not mustered the will, nor the vision to create a lasting and fundamental change.

PLANETARY CONSCIOUSNESS

In light of today's global crises, humankind has begun to seek new avenues and modes of thinking. Such modes are the ancient, albeit very pertinent, indigenous wisdoms. To them, planetary consciousness is not merely an ancillary notion, but their very essence. When we study these modes, we realize that the new planetary consciousness is actually an old, perennial consciousness; only now it is being rediscovered.

Indeed, it is high time that planetary consciousness was rediscovered. We used to think that the typical, "normal" human consciousness is what we capture with our five senses. We considered everything else imaginary. The common perception was that we ended where our skin ended. Other views were considered "new age," "mystical," or "esoteric." Ideas that we somehow belong together, that there is a context in which we are parts of a greater whole, have been considered the exception in the history of civilization.

But if we look at the history of ideas, we will find that the truth is quite the opposite. The reductionist, mechanistic, and fragmented thinking that evolved in the Western world over the last 300 years is not the norm, but the exception. Other cultures do not share this view. Even the West did not adhere to it prior to the emergence of the mechanistic worldview that it inherited as an application (or rather, misapplication) of Newton's philosophy of nature.

In other cultures, as well as in the Western world preceding modern times, the prevailing consciousness was one of belonging, of oneness. Most traditional cultures do not agree that people have nothing in common but passing interests that happen to coincide.

The classical roots of all the wisdom traditions are concepts of a "planetary consciousness." This term defines the awareness of our shared fate as human beings, as citizens of this planet. If we are to sustain our existence, if we are to ensure that our children and grandchildren have a secure and sustainable future, we *must* foster a planetary consciousness.

To move forward, we must cultivate a mindset that enables us to form a united human family, a planetary civilization. However, this civilization should not be a monolithic culture where everyone follows the same ideas, and one person or nation dictates those ideas to everybody else. Rather, it should be a diverse civilization whose elements join together to maintain and develop the whole system, the planetary civilization of humankind.

This diversity is the element of harmony, the element of peace. Every society that has survived has possessed it. Only Western and westernized societies have forgotten it. In the process of creating technical and economic progress, they have fragmented the integrity, the oneness of the system. It is high time we restore it.

As I learned through my acquaintance with Dr. Laitman's writings, Kabbalah in its authentic form not only promotes the concept of oneness and the integrity of humanity and the universe, it also offers practical measures to restore it when lost.

It is my heartfelt recommendation to read carefully through this book, as it provides much more than general knowledge about an ancient wisdom. It also provides a key to ensure the well-being of humanity in these critical times, when we face the unprecedented challenge of choosing between the *devolutionary* path leading to worldwide breakdown, and the *evolutionary* path that can bring us to a world of peace, harmony, well-being, and sustainability.

Ervin Laszlo

1
KABBALAH: THEN AND NOW

THE MASTER PLAN

It is no secret that Kabbalah did not begin with today's Hollywood trendy hype. It has actually been around for thousands of years. When it first appeared, people were much closer to Nature than they are today. They felt an intimacy with Nature and nurtured their relationship with it.

In those days, they had little reason to be detached from Nature. They weren't as self-centered and alienated from their natural environment as we are today. Indeed, at that time, humanity was an inseparable part of Nature and nurtured its intimacy with it.

In addition, humankind did not know enough about Nature to feel secure; instead, we were afraid of natural forces, which impelled us to relate to Nature as a force superior to our own.

Being intimate with Nature, on the one hand, and afraid of it, on the other hand, people aspired not only to learn about their surrounding world, but even more important, to determine what or who governed it.

In those early days, people couldn't hide from Nature's elements as they do today; they couldn't avoid its hardships as we do in our "manmade" world. And most important, the fear of Nature, and at the same time, the closeness to it, urged many to search for and discover Nature's plan for them, and coincidentally, for all of us.

Those pioneers in Nature's research wanted to know if Nature actually had a goal, and if so, what humanity's role might be in this Master Plan. Those individuals who received the highest level of knowledge, that of the Master Plan, are known as "Kabbalists."

A unique individual among those pioneers was Abraham. When he discovered the Master Plan, he not only researched it in depth, but first and foremost taught it to others. He realized that the only guarantee against misery and fear was for people to fully understand Nature's plan for them. And once he realized this, he spared no effort teaching whoever wished to learn. For this reason, Abraham became the first Kabbalist to start a dynasty of Kabbalah teachers: The most worthy students became the next generation of teachers, who then passed on the knowledge to the next generation of students.

Kabbalists refer to the designer of the Master Plan as "the Creator," and to the Plan itself as "The Thought of Creation." In other words, and this is important, when

Kabbalists talk about Nature or Nature's laws, they are
talking about the Creator. And vise versa, when they are
talking about the Creator, they are talking about Nature
or Nature's laws. These terms are synonymous.

The term, "Kabbalist," comes from the Hebrew
word, Kabbalah ("reception"). The original language of Kabbalah is Hebrew, a language developed especially by and for Kabbalists, to help them communicate
with one another about spiritual matters. Many Kabbalah
books have been written in other languages, too, but the
basic terms are always in Hebrew.

To a Kabbalist, the term, "Creator," does not signify a supernatural, distinct entity, but the next degree
that a human being should reach when pursuing higher
knowledge. The Hebrew word for Creator is *Boreh,* and
contains two words: *Bo* (come) and *Re'eh* (see). Thus, the
word, "Creator," is a personal invitation to experience
the spiritual world.

THE CRADLE OF SCIENCE

The knowledge that the first Kabbalists acquired did
more than help them understand how things worked
behind the scenes. With it, they were able to explain
the natural phenomena we all encounter. It was only
natural, therefore, that they became teachers, and that
the knowledge they passed on to us became the basis for
both ancient and modern sciences.

Perhaps we think of Kabbalists as secluded people hiding in dim, candle-lit chambers, writing magical scriptures. Well, until the end of the 20th century, Kabbalah was indeed kept secret. The clandestine approach toward Kabbalah evoked numerous tales and legends surrounding its nature. Although most of these tales are false, they still baffle and confuse even the most rigorous thinkers.

Gottfried Leibnitz, a great mathematician and philosopher, candidly expressed his thoughts on how secrecy had affected Kabbalah: "Because man did not have the right key to the secret, the thirst for knowledge was ultimately reduced to all sorts of trivia and superstitions that brought forward a sort of 'vulgar Kabbalah' that has little in common with the true Kabbalah, as well as various fantasies under the false name of magic, and this is what fills the books."

But Kabbalah was not always secret. In fact, the first Kabbalists were very open about their knowledge, and at the same time, very much involved with their societies. Often, Kabbalists were their nation's leaders. Of all these leaders, King David is probably the best known example of a great Kabbalist who was also a great leader.

The involvement of Kabbalists in their societies helped their contemporary scholars develop the basis of what we now know as "Western philosophy," which later became the basis of modern science. In that regard, here's what Johannes Reuchlin, a humanist, classics scholar, and expert in ancient languages and traditions, writes in his book, *De Arte Cabbalistica*: "My teacher, Pythagoras, the father of philosophy, took his teaching from Kabbalists ... He was the first to translate the word, *Kabbalah*, unknown to his contemporaries, to the Greek word *philosophy*... Kabbalah does not let us live our lives in the dust, but elevates our mind to the height of knowledge."

OTHER ROUTES

But philosophers were not Kabbalists. Because they did not study Kabbalah, they couldn't fully understand the depth of Kabbalistic knowledge. As a result, knowledge that should have been developed and treated in a very specific way was developed and treated incorrectly. When Kabbalistic knowledge migrated to other parts of the world, where there were no Kabbalists at the time, it also took a different course.

Thus, humanity made a detour. Although Western philosophy incorporated parts of the Kabbalistic knowledge, it ended up taking an entirely different direction. Western philosophy generated sciences that researched our material world, that which we perceive with our five senses. But Kabbalah is a science that studies what happens *beyond* what our senses perceive. The changed emphasis drove humanity in the opposite direction from the original knowledge that Kabbalists obtained. This change in direction took humanity on a detour whose consequences we will explore in the following chapter.

THE BIG QUESTIONS

Kabbalah became hidden about 2,000 years ago. The reason was simple—there was no demand for it. Since that time, humanity has occupied itself with developing monotheistic religions, and later on, science. Both were created to answer man's most fundamental questions: "What is our place in the world, in the universe?" What is the purpose of our existence?" In other words, "Why were we born?"

But today, more than ever before, many people feel that what has worked for 2,000 years no longer meets their needs. The answers provided by religion and science no longer satisfy them. These people are looking elsewhere for answers to the most basic questions about the purpose of life. They turn to Eastern teachings, fortune-telling, magic and mysticism. And some turn to Kabbalah.

Because Kabbalah was formulated to answer these fundamental questions, the answers it provides are directly related to them. By rediscovering ancient answers about the meaning of life, we are literally mending the rupture between humanity and Nature that occurred when we turned away from Kabbalah and toward philosophy.

KABBALAH STEPS IN

Kabbalah made its "debut" about 5,000 years ago in Mesopotamia, an ancient country in today's Iraq. Mesopotamia was not only the birthplace of Kabbalah, but of all ancient teachings and mysticism. In those days, people believed in many different teachings, often following more than one teaching at a time. Astrology, fortune-telling, numerology, magic, witchcraft, spells, evil eye—all those and more were developed and thrived in Mesopotamia, the cultural center of the ancient world.

As long as people were happy with their beliefs, they felt no need for change. People wanted to know that their lives would be safe, and what they needed to do to make them enjoyable. They were not asking about the origin of life, or most important, who or what had created the rules of life.

At first, this may seem like a slight difference. But actually, the difference between asking about life, and asking about the rules that shape life, is like the difference between learning how to drive a car and learning how to make one. It's a totally different level of knowledge.

THE ENGINE OF CHANGE

Desires don't just pop out of the blue. They form unconsciously within us and surface only when they become something definable, such as, "I want a pizza." Before that, desires are either not felt, or at most, felt as general restlessness. We've all experienced that sense of wanting something but not quite knowing what it is. Well, it is a desire that has not yet ripened.

Plato once said, "Necessity is the mother of invention," and he was right. Similarly, Kabbalah teaches us that the only way we can learn anything is by first wanting to learn it. It's a very simple formula: when we want something, we do what it takes to get it. We make the time, muster the energy, and develop the necessary skills. It turns out that the engine of change is desire.

The way our desires evolve both defines and designs the entire history of humanity. As humankind's desires developed, they urged people to study their environment so they could fulfill their wishes. Unlike minerals, plants, and animals, people constantly evolve. For every generation, and for each person, desires grow stronger and stronger.

TAKING THE DRIVER'S SEAT

This engine of change—desire—is made of five levels, zero through four. Kabbalists refer to this engine as "a will to receive pleasure," or simply, "the will to receive." When Kabbalah first appeared, some 5,000 years ago, the will to receive was at level zero. Today, as you might have guessed, we are at level four—the most intense level.

But in the early days when the will to receive was at level zero, desires were not strong enough to separate us from Nature and from each other. In those days, this oneness with Nature, which today many of us pay good money to re-learn in meditation classes (and let's face it, not always successfully) was the natural way of life. People didn't know any other way. They didn't even know that they could be separated from Nature, nor did they want to be.

In fact, in those days, humanity's communication with Nature and with each other flowed so seamlessly, words were not even necessary; instead, people communicated by thought, much like telepathy. It was a time of unity, and the whole of humanity was like a single nation.

But while still in Mesopotamia, a change occurred: people's desires started to grow and they became more egoistic. People began to want to change Nature and use it for themselves. Instead of wanting to adapt themselves to Nature, they began wanting to change Nature to fit *their* needs. They grew detached from Nature, separated and alienated from it and from each other. Today, many, many centuries later, we are discovering that this was not a good idea. It simply doesn't work.

Naturally, as people began to place themselves in opposition to their environment and their societies, they no longer related to others as kin and to Nature as home. Hatred replaced love, and people grew apart and became detached from one another.

In consequence, the single nation of the ancient world was divided. It first split into two groups that drifted to the east and to the west. The two groups continued to divide and splinter, eventually forming the multitude of nations we have today.

One of the most obvious symptoms of the division, which the Bible describes as "The Fall of the Tower of Babel," was the creation of different languages. These different languages disconnected people from each other and created confusion and malfunction. The Hebrew word for confusion is *Bilbul*, and to mark the confusion, the capital of Mesopotamia received the name, Babel (Babylon).

Ever since that split—when our desires grew from level zero to level one—we have been confronting Nature. Instead of correcting the ever-growing egoism to remain as one with Nature, that is, with the Creator, we have built a mechanical, technological shield to protect us from it. The initial reason we developed science and technology was to secure our shielded existence away from Nature's elements. It turns out, however, that whether we are aware of it or not, we are actually trying to control the Creator and take over the driver's seat.

At the time when all this *Bilbul* was taking place, Abraham was living in Babylon, helping his father build little idols and sell them in the family shop. It's not hard to see that Abraham was right in the middle of all this vibrant mishmash of ideas that thrived in Babylon, the New York of the ancient world. This confusion also explains Abraham's persistent question, whose answer led him to discover Nature's law: "Who is the owner of the capital?" When he realized that there was a purpose to the confusion and the alienation, he quickly taught it to whomever was willing to listen.

HIDING, SEEKING, BUT NOT FINDING

The level of egoism in humanity has kept growing, with each level driving us farther away from Nature (the Creator). In Kabbalah, distance is not measured in inches or yards; it's measured in *qualities*. The Creator's quality is wholeness, connectedness, and giving, but it is only possible to feel Him when we share His qualities. If I am self-centered, there is no way I can connect to anything as whole and altruistic as the Creator. It would be like trying to see another person when we are standing back to back.

Because we are standing back to back with the Creator and because we still want to control Him, clearly, the more we try, the more frustrated we become. Certainly, we cannot control something we can't see or even feel. This desire can never be filled unless we make a U-turn, look in the opposite direction, and find Him.

Many people are already growing tired of technology's broken promises of wealth, health, and most important, safe tomorrows. Too few people have attained all these today, and even they cannot be certain they will still have them tomorrow. But the benefit of this state is that it forces us to reexamine our direction and ask, "Is it possible we've been treading the wrong path all along?"

Particularly today, as we acknowledge the crisis and the impasse we are facing, we can openly admit that the path we've chosen is a dead-end street. Instead of compensating for our self-centered oppositeness from Nature by choosing technology, we should have changed our egoism to altruism, and consequently to unity with Nature.

In Kabbalah, the term used for this change is *Tik-kun* (correction). To realize our oppositeness from the Creator means that we must acknowledge the split that occurred among us (human beings) five thousand years ago. This is called "the recognition of evil." It is not easy, but it is the first step to true health and happiness.

THE GLOBAL CRISIS HAS A HAPPY END

Over the past 5,000 years, each of the two factions that tore from Mesopotamia evolved into a civilization of many different peoples. Of the two primary groups, one became what we refer to as "Western civilization," and the other became what we know as "Eastern civilization."

The worsening clash between the two civilizations reflects the culmination of the process that began at the first division. Five thousand years ago, a single nation was divided because egoism grew and separated its members. Now it is time for this "nation"—humanity—to reunite and become a single nation once again. We are still at the breaking point that occurred all those years ago, but today we are much more aware of it.

According to the wisdom of Kabbalah, this culture clash and the resurfacing of mystical beliefs that were abundant in ancient Mesopotamia mark the beginning of humanity's reconnection into a new civilization. Today, we are beginning to realize that we are all connected and that we must rebuild the state that existed prior to the shattering. By rebuilding into a united humanity, we will also rebuild our connection with Nature, with the Creator.

EGOISM IS A CATCH-22

During the time when mysticism thrived, the wisdom of Kabbalah was discovered and provided knowledge about the stage-by-stage growth of our egoism and what causes it. Kabbalists taught that everything that exists is made of a desire for self-fulfillment.

However, these desires cannot be fulfilled in their natural form, when they are self-centered. This is because when we satisfy a desire, we cancel it, and if we cancel a desire for something, we can no longer enjoy it.

For example, think of your favorite food. Now, imagine yourself in a fancy restaurant, comfortably seated at a table as the smiling waiter brings you a covered plate, places it in front of you, and removes the lid. Hmmm... that deliciously familiar scent! Enjoying yourself yet? Your body does; that's why it releases digestive juices at the mere thought of this dish.

But the minute you start eating, the pleasure diminishes. The fuller you become, the less pleasure you derive from eating. Finally, when you've had your fill, you can no longer enjoy the food, and you stop eating. You don't stop because you're full, but because eating is no fun on a full stomach. This is the Catch-22 of egoism—if you have what you want, you no longer want it.

Therefore, because we cannot live without pleasure, we *must* go on searching for new and greater pleasures. We do that by developing new desires, which will also remain unfulfilled. It's a vicious circle. Clearly, the more we want, the emptier we feel. And the emptier we feel, the more frustrated we become.

And because we are now at the most intense level of desire in our history, we cannot avoid the conclusion that today we are more dissatisfied than ever before, even though we clearly have more than our fathers and our forefathers had. The contrast between what we have, on the one hand, and our growing dissatisfaction, on the other hand, is the essence of the crisis we are experiencing today. The more egoistic we become, the emptier we feel, and the worse is the crisis.

THE NECESSITY OF ALTRUISM

Originally, all people were internally connected. We felt and thought of ourselves as a single human being, and this is exactly how Nature treats us. This "collective" human being is called "Adam," from the Hebrew word, *Domeh* (similar), meaning similar to the Creator, who is also single and whole. However, despite our initial oneness, as our egoism grew we gradually lost the sensation of unity and became increasingly distant from each other.

Kabbalah books write that Nature's plan is for our egoism to keep growing until we realize that we have become separated and hateful to one another. The logic behind the plan is that we must first feel as a single entity, and then become separated into egoistic and detached individuals. Only then will we realize that we are completely opposite from the Creator, and utterly selfish.

Moreover, this is the only way for us to realize that egoism is negative, unfulfilling, and ultimately hopeless. As we have said, our egoism separates us from each other and from Nature. But to change that, we must first realize that this is the case. This will bring us to want to change, and to independently find a way to transform ourselves into altruists, reconnected with all of humanity and with Nature—the Creator. After all, we have already said that desire is the engine of change.

Kabbalist Yehuda Ashlag writes that the entrance of the Upper Light into the desire and its departure from it, make a vessel fit for its task: altruistic. In other words, if we want to feel unity with the Creator, we must first be united with Him, then experience the loss of this unity. By experiencing both states we will be able to make a conscious choice, and consciousness is necessary for true unity.

We can compare this process to a child who feels connected to its parents as a baby, rebels as an adolescent, and finally, as the child becomes an adult, understands and justifies his or her upbringing.

Actually, altruism is not an option. It just seems as if we can choose whether to be egoistic or altruistic. But if we examine Nature, we will find that altruism is the most fundamental law of nature. For example, each cell in the body is inherently egoistic. But to exist, it must relinquish its egoistic tendencies for the sake of the body's well-being. The reward for that cell is that it experiences not only its own existence, but the life of the whole body.

We, too, must develop a similar connection with each other. Then, the more successful we become at bonding, the more we will feel Adam's eternal existence instead of our passing physical existence.

Especially today, altruism has become essential for our survival. It has become evident that we are all connected and dependent on one another. This dependency produces a new and very precise definition of altruism: Any act or intention that comes from a need to connect humanity into a single entity is considered altruistic. Conversely, any act or intention that is *not* focused on uniting humanity is egoistic.

It follows that our oppositeness from Nature is the source of all the suffering we are seeing in the world. Everything else in Nature—minerals, plants, and animals—instinctively follow Nature's altruistic law. Only human behavior is in contrast with the rest of Nature and with the Creator.

Moreover, the suffering we see around us is not just our own. All other parts of Nature also suffer from our wrongful actions. If every part of Nature instinctively follows its law, and if only man does not, then man is the only corrupted element in Nature. Simply put, when we correct ourselves from egoism to altruism, everything else will be corrected, as well—ecology, famine, war, and society at large.

ENHANCED PERCEPTION

There is a special bonus to altruism. It may seem as if the only change will be putting others before ourselves, but there are actually far greater benefits. When we begin to think of others, we become integrated with them, and they with us.

Think of it this way: There are about 6.5 billion people in the world today. What if, instead of having two hands, two legs, and one brain to control them, you had 13 billion hands, 13 billion legs, and 6.5 billion brains to control them? Sounds confusing? Not really, because all those brains would function as a single brain, and the hands would function as a single pair of hands. All of humanity would function as one body whose capabilities are enhanced 6.5 billion times.

Wait, we're not done with the bonuses! In addition to becoming superhuman, anyone who becomes altruistic will also receive the most desirable gift of all: omniscience, or total recall and total knowledge. Because altruism is the Creator's nature, acquiring it equalizes our nature with His, and we begin to *think* like Him. We begin to know why everything happens, when it should happen, and what to do should we want to make it happen differently. In Kabbalah, this state is called "equivalence of form," and this is the purpose of Creation.

This state of enhanced perception, of equivalence of form, is why we were created in the first place. This is why we were created united and were then broken—so we could reunite. In the process of uniting, we will learn why Nature does what it does, and become as wise as the Thought that created it.

When we unite with Nature, we will feel as eternal and complete as Nature. In that state, even when our bodies die, we will feel that we continue to exist in the eternal Nature. Physical life and death will no longer affect us because our previous self-centered perception will have been replaced with a whole, altruistic perception. Our own lives will have become the life of the whole of Nature.

THE TIME IS NOW

The Book of Zohar, the "Bible" of Kabbalah, was written approximately 2,000 years ago. It states that toward the end of the 20th century, humankind's egoism will soar to unprecedented intensity.

As we have seen before, the more we want, the emptier we feel. Therefore, since the end of the 20th century, humanity has been experiencing its worst emptiness ever. *The Book of Zohar* also writes that when this emptiness is felt, humanity will need a means to cure it and to help people become fulfilled. Then, says *The Zohar*, the time will come to present Kabbalah to all of humanity as a means of acquiring fulfillment through similarity with Nature.

The process of acquiring fulfillment, the *Tikkun*, will not happen all at once and not simultaneously for everyone. For a *Tikkun* to occur, a person must *want* it to happen. It is a process that evolves out of one's own volition.

Correction begins when a person realizes that his or her egoistic nature is the source of all evil. It is a very personal and powerful experience, but it invariably brings one to want to change, move from egoism to altruism.

As we have said, the Creator treats all of us as a single, united created being. We have tried to achieve our goals egoistically, but today we are discovering that our problems will only be solved collectively and altruistically. The more conscious we become of our egoism, the more we will want to use the method of Kabbalah to change our nature to altruism. We did not do it when Kabbalah first appeared, but we can do it now, because now we know we need it!

The past 5,000 years of human evolution have been a process of trying one method, examining the pleasures it provides, becoming disillusioned with it, and leaving it for another. Methods came and went, but we have not grown happier. Now that the method of Kabbalah has appeared, aimed to correct the highest level of egoism, we no longer have to tread the path of disillusionment. We can simply correct our worst egoism through Kabbalah, and all other corrections will follow like a domino effect. Thus, during this correction, we can feel fulfillment, inspiration, and joy.

IN A NUTSHELL

The wisdom of Kabbalah (the wisdom of reception) first appeared about 5,000 years ago, when humans began to ask about the purpose of their existence. Those who knew it were called "Kabbalists," and had the answer to life's purpose and to the role of humanity in the universe.

But in those days, the desires of most people were too small to strive for this knowledge. So when Kabbalists saw that humanity did not need their wisdom, they hid it and secretly prepared it for a time when everyone would be ready for it. In the meantime, humanity cultivated other channels such as religion and science.

Today, when growing numbers of people are convinced that religion and science do not provide the answers to life's deepest questions, they are beginning to look elsewhere for answers. This is the time that Kabbalah has been waiting for, and this is why it is reappearing—to provide the answer to the purpose of existence.

Kabbalah tells us that Nature, which is synonymous with the Creator, is whole, altruistic, and united. It tells us that we must not only understand Nature, but we must also want to implement this manner of existence within ourselves.

Kabbalah also tells us that by so doing we will not only equalize with Nature, we will understand the Thought that stands behind it—the Master Plan. Finally, Kabbalah states that by understanding the Master Plan, we will become equal to the Master Planner, and that this is the purpose of Creation—to equalize with the Creator.

2

THE GREATEST WISH OF ALL

Now that we've been introduced to the origins of Kabbalah, it's time to see how Kabbalah relates to us.

As many of you may already know, the study of Kabbalah introduces a great many foreign terms, most of which come from Hebrew, some from Aramaic, and some from other languages, such as Greek. But here's the good news: beginners, and even intermediate students, can do just fine with only a few of these terms. Although they signify spiritual states, if you experience them within, you will also discover their correct names.

Kabbalah talks about desires and how to satisfy them. It has researched the human soul and its growth from its humble beginning as a spiritual seed to its culmination as the Tree of Life. Once you get the gist of it, you'll learn the rest within your own heart.

SPRINGBOARD
FOR GROWTH

Let's start where we ended the first chapter. We said that things could be great if we would only learn to use our egoism differently—to bond with others so as to form a single spiritual being. We even learned that there's a means for it—the method of Kabbalah, devised for just that purpose.

But if we look around, we can clearly see that we are not headed for a positive future. We're in a crisis—a big one. Even if we haven't been harmed by it, we have no guarantee we will remain unharmed. It appears that there is no area where the crisis has not left its mark, whether in our personal lives, the societies we live in, or in Nature.

Crises in and of themselves are not necessarily negative; they simply indicate that the present state of things has exhausted itself, and that it's time to move on to the next phase. Democracy, the industrial revolution, women's liberation, quantum physics, all of these appeared as results of crises in their fields. In fact, everything that exists today is the result of a past crisis.

Today's crisis is not essentially different from previous ones; it is, however, far more intense, affecting the entire world. But like any crisis, it is an opportunity for change, a springboard for growth. If we choose correctly, all hardships could simply vanish. We could easily provide food, water, and shelter for the entire world. We could establish world peace and make this world a thriving, dynamic planet. But for that to happen, we must *want* to make it happen and choose what Nature *wants* us to choose—unity, instead of our present choice of separation.

Why, then, don't we want to connect? Why are we alienating each other? The more we progress and the more knowledge we gain, the more discontented we become. We've learned how to build spaceships, how to build molecule-size robots; we have deciphered the entire human genome. Why then haven't we learned how to be happy?

The more we'll learn about Kabbalah, the more we'll find that it always leads us to the root of things. Before it gives you any answers, it tells you why you are in your present state. And once you know the root of your situation, you will rarely need any further guidance. In that spirit, let's see what we have been learning until today, and perhaps we will discover why we still haven't discovered the key to happiness.

BEHIND CLOSED DOORS

> Man... if he be insufficiently or ill-educated,
> he is the most savage of earthly creatures.
>
> —Plato, The Laws

Knowledge has always been considered an asset. Espionage is not an invention of modern times; it has been there since the dawn of history. But it has existed because knowledge has always been disclosed on a need-to-know basis, and the only dispute was about *who* needs to know.

In the past, the knowledgeable ones were called "sages," and the knowledge they possessed was of Nature's secrets. The sages hid their knowledge, fearing it might fall into the hands of those whom they considered unworthy.

But how do we determine who is entitled to know? Does the fact that I have some exclusive piece of information give me the right to hide it? Naturally, no person would agree that he or she is unworthy of knowing; hence we try to "steal" whatever information we want, and which isn't openly accessible.

But that wasn't always the case. Many years ago, before egoism reached its highest level, people considered the public's benefit before they considered their own. They felt connected to the whole of Nature and to the whole of humanity, not to themselves. For them, this was the natural way to be.

But today, our considerations have changed drastically, and we believe that we are entitled to know everything and to do everything. This is what our level of egoism automatically dictates.

In fact, even before humanity reached the fourth level of desire, scholars had begun to sell their wisdom for material profits such as money, honor, and power. As material temptations grew, people could no longer keep to their modest way of life and turn their efforts entirely to researching Nature. Instead, these wise people began to use their knowledge to gain material pleasures.

Today, with the progress of technology and the heightened drive of our egos, misusing knowledge has become the norm. Yet, the more technology progresses, the more dangerous we are becoming to ourselves and to our surroundings. As we become more powerful, we are more tempted to use our power to get what we want.

As we have said before, the will to receive consists of four levels of intensity. The more powerful it becomes, the greater our social and moral decline. It is, therefore, no wonder that we're in a crisis. It is also very clear why sages hid their knowledge, and why their own growing egoism now compels them to disclose it.

Without changing ourselves, knowledge and progress will not help us. They will only produce greater harm than they already have. Therefore, it would be grossly naive to expect scientific advancement to keep its promise of a good life. If we want a brighter future, we need only change ourselves.

THE EVOLUTION OF DESIRES

The statement that human nature is egoistic is unlikely to make any headlines. But because we are naturally egoistic, we are all, without exception, prone to misusing what we know. This need not mean that we will use knowledge to commit a crime. It can express itself in very small, seemingly trifle things, like getting promoted at work when we didn't deserve it, or taking our best friend's loved one away from them.

The real news about egoism is not that human nature is egoistic; it is that *I am an egoist*. The first time we confront our own egoism is quite a sobering experience. And like any sobering, it is a giant headache.

There is good reason why our will to receive constantly evolves, and we will touch upon it in a little while. But for now, let's focus on the role of this evolution in how we acquire knowledge.

When a new desire appears, it creates new needs. And when we search for ways to satisfy these needs, we develop and improve our minds. In other words, it is the evolution of the will to receive pleasure that creates evolution.

A look at human history from the perspective of the evolution of desires shows how these growing desires generated every concept, discovery, and invention. Each innovation, in fact, has been a tool that helps us satisfy the mounting needs and demands our desires create.

The first level of desire relates to physical desires such as food, sex, family, and home. These are the most elementary desires, shared by all living creatures.

Unlike the first level of desires, all other levels are uniquely human and stem from being in a human society. The second level is the desire for wealth; the third is the desire for honor, fame and domination, and the fourth level is the desire for knowledge.

Happiness or unhappiness, and pleasure or suffering depend on how much we satisfy our needs. But satisfaction requires effort. Actually, we are so pleasure-driven that, according to Kabbalist Yehuda Ashlag, "One cannot perform even the slightest movement without motivation ... without somehow benefiting oneself." Moreover, "When, for example, one moves one's hand from the chair to the table it is because one thinks that by putting one's hand on the table one will receive greater pleasure. If one did not think so, one would leave one's hand on the chair for the rest of one's life."

In the previous chapter, we said that egoism is a Catch-22. In other words, the intensity of the pleasure depends on the intensity of the desire. As satiation increases, desire proportionally decreases. Therefore, when the desire is gone, so is the pleasure. It turns out that to enjoy something, we must not only want it, but keep wanting it, or the pleasure will fade away.

Moreover, the pleasure is not in the desired object; it's in the one who wants the pleasure. For example: If I'm crazy about tuna, it doesn't mean that the tuna has any pleasure within it, but that a pleasure in the "form" of tuna exists in *me*.

Ask any tuna if it enjoys its own flesh. I doubt it would answer positively. I might tactlessly ask the tuna, "But why aren't you enjoying it? When I take a bite of you, it tastes so good... And you have tons of tuna! If I were you, I'd be in Heaven."

Of course, we all know this is not a realistic dialogue, and not just because tuna don't speak English. We instinctively feel that tuna fish can't enjoy their own flesh, while humans can very much enjoy the taste of tuna.

Why this human enjoyment of the taste of tuna? *Because we have a desire for it.* The reason tuna fish can't enjoy their own flesh is that they have no desire for it. A specific desire to receive pleasure from a specific object is called a *Kli* (vessel/tool), and reception of pleasure within the *Kli* is called *Ohr* (Light). The concept of the *Kli* and *Ohr* is unquestionably the most important concept in the wisdom of Kabbalah. When you can build a *Kli*, a vessel for the Creator, you will receive His Light.

HANDLING DESIRES

Now that we know that desires generate progress, let's see how we've handled them throughout history. For the most part, we've had two ways of manipulating desires:

1. Turning everything into habits, "taming" desires, or harnessing them into a daily routine;

2. Diminishing and suppressing them.

Most religions use the first option, "tagging" each act with a reward. To motivate us to do what is considered good, our tutors and those around us reward us with positive feedback whenever we do something "right." As we grow older, the rewards gradually stop, but our actions have become "tagged" in our minds as rewarding.

Once we are used to something, it becomes second nature to us. And when we act according to our nature, we always feel comfortable with ourselves.

The second way to handle our desires—by diminishing them—is primarily used by Eastern teachings. This approach follows a simple rule: Better to not want, than to want and not have, or in the words of Lao-tzu (604 BC - 531 BC), "Manifest plainness; embrace simplicity; reduce selfishness; have few desires" (*The Way of Lao-tzu*).

For many years, it seemed that we were getting by with just these two methods. Although we did not get what we wanted—because of the rule that when you have what you want, you no longer want it—the chase itself was gratifying. Whenever a new desire came along, we believed that this one would surely fulfill our wishes. We were hopeful as long as we kept dreaming; and where there is hope, there is life, even without actually fulfilling those dreams.

But our desires grew. They have become increasingly hard to satisfy with unfulfilled dreams, with an empty *Kli*, devoid of the filling it was meant to have. And thus, the two ways—taming desires and diminishing them—are facing a major challenge. When we can't diminish our desires, we have no choice but to look for a way to satisfy them. In that state, we either abandon the old ways, or somehow combine them with a new way of searching.

A NEW DESIRE IN TOWN

We have said that there are four degrees to the will to receive: a) physical desires for food, reproduction, and family; b) wealth; c) power and respect, sometimes separated into two distinct groups; and d) the desire for knowledge.

The four degrees are divided into two groups: 1) animal desires, the first degree, are shared by all living creatures; and 2) human desires, degrees two, three, and four, which are uniquely human. The latter group is the one that's brought us to where we are today.

But today there is a new desire—the fifth degree in the evolution of the will to receive. As we've said in the previous chapter, *The Book of Zohar* writes that at the end of the 20th century a new desire will appear.

This new desire is not just another desire; it is the culmination of all the degrees of desires preceding it. It is not only the most powerful desire, but it contains unique features that differentiate it from all other desires.

When Kabbalists talk about the heart, they aren't referring to the physical heart, but to desires of the first four degrees. But the fifth level of desire is essentially different. It wants satisfaction only from spirituality, not from anything physical. This desire is also the root of the spiritual growth one is destined to experience. For this reason, Kabbalists call this desire the "point in the heart."

A NEW METHOD FOR A NEW DESIRE

When the "point in the heart" appears, one begins to shift from wanting worldly pleasures—sex, money, power, and knowledge—to wanting spiritual pleasures. Because this is a new kind of pleasure that we're seeking, we also need a new method to satisfy it. The method to satisfy the new desire is called "the wisdom of Kabbalah" (the wisdom of how to receive).

To understand this new method, let's look at the difference between the wisdom of Kabbalah, whose aim is to fulfill the desire for spirituality, and the methods used to fulfill all other desires. With our "ordinary" desires, we can usually define what we want quite easily. If I want to eat, I look for food; if I want respect, I act in a way that I believe will make people respect me.

But because I don't quite know what spirituality is, how can I know what to do to attain it? Because in the beginning, we don't realize that what we really want is to discover the Creator, we also don't realize that we will need a new method to search for Him. This desire is so utterly different from anything we've ever felt before, it is unclear even to us. This is why the method of discovering and satisfying it is designated "The Wisdom of the Hidden."

As long as all we wanted was food, social status, and—at most, knowledge—we didn't need The Wisdom of the Hidden. We had no use for it, so it remained hidden. But its concealment does not mean that it was abandoned. On the contrary, for five thousand years Kabbalists have been polishing and refining it for the time when people would need it. They have been writing simpler and simpler books to make Kabbalah understandable and more accessible.

They knew that in the future the whole world would need it, and they wrote that this would happen when the fifth level of desire appeared. Now this level has appeared, and those who recognize it feel the need for the wisdom of Kabbalah.

In Kabbalistic terms: To receive pleasure, you must have a *Kli* for it, a well-defined desire for a very specific pleasure. The appearance of a *Kli* forces our brains to search for a way to fill it with *Ohr* (Light). Now that many of us have "points in our hearts," the wisdom of Kabbalah presents itself as a means to satisfy our desire for spirituality.

TIKKUN–THE CORRECTION
OF THE WILL TO RECEIVE

We have already said that the will to receive is a Catch-22: when I finally receive what I've been looking for, I almost immediately stop wanting it. And of course, without wanting it, I cannot enjoy it.

The desire for spirituality comes with its own pre-installed, unique mechanism to avoid this catch. This mechanism is called *Tikkun* (correction). A desire of the fifth level must first be "coated" with this *Tikkun* before it can be used efficiently and pleasurably.

Understanding the *Tikkun* will solve many common misunderstandings about Kabbalah. The will to receive has been the driving force behind every progress and change in the history of humanity. But the desire to receive has always been one to receive pleasure for self-gratification. While there is nothing wrong with wanting to receive pleasure, the *intention* to enjoy for self-gratification places us in opposition to Nature, the Creator. Therefore, by wanting to receive *for ourselves* we are separating ourselves from the Creator. This is our corruption, the reason for every misfortune and discontentment.

A *Tikkun* happens not when we stop receiving, but when we change the reason for which we are receiving, our *intention*. When we receive for ourselves, it is called "egoism." When we receive in order to unite with the Creator, it is called "altruism," meaning unity with Nature.

For example, would you enjoy eating the same food every day for months? Probably not. But this is exactly what babies are required to do. They have no choice in the matter. In fact, the only reason they agree to it is because they don't know anything else. But surely there is only so much pleasure they can derive from eating, other than filling their empty stomachs.

Now, think of the baby's mother. Imagine her face glowing as she is feeding her child. She is in heaven just watching her child eat healthily. The baby may (at most) be content, but the mother is elated.

Here's what happens: Both the mother and the child enjoy the child's desire for food. But while the child's focus is on its own stomach, the mother's pleasure is infinitely greater because of her delight in giving to her baby. Her focus is not on herself, but on her child.

It is the same with Nature. If we knew what Nature wanted of us, and fulfilled it, we would feel the pleasure of giving. Moreover, we would not feel it on the instinctive level that mothers naturally experience with their babies, but on the spiritual level of our bond with Nature.

In Hebrew—the original language of Kabbalah—an intention is called *Kavana*. Therefore, the *Tikkun* we need is to place the right *Kavana* over our desires. The reward for making a *Tikkun* and having a *Kavana* is the fulfillment of the last, the greatest of all wishes—the desire for spirituality, for the Creator. When this desire is fulfilled, one knows the system that controls reality, participates in its making, and eventually receives the keys and sits in the driver's seat. Such a person will no longer experience life and death the way we do, but will effortlessly and joyfully flow through eternity in a never-ending stream of bliss and wholeness, united with the Creator.

IN A NUTSHELL

There are five levels to our desires, divided into three groups. The first group is animal desires (food, reproduction, and home); the second is human desires (money, honor, knowledge), and the third group is the spiritual desire (the "point in the heart").

As long as only the first two groups were active, we settled for "taming" our desires through routine, and for suppressing them. When the "point in the heart" appeared, the first two ways no longer did the job, and we had to look for another way. This is when the wisdom of Kabbalah resurfaced, after having been hidden for thousands of years, waiting for the time it would be needed.

The wisdom of Kabbalah is the means for our *Tikkun* (correction). Using it, we can change our *Kavana* (intention) from wanting self-gratification, defined as egoism, to wanting to gratify the whole of Nature, the Creator, defined as altruism.

The global crisis we are experiencing today is really a crisis of desires. When we use the wisdom of Kabbalah to satisfy the last, greatest wish of all—the desire for spirituality—all problems will be resolved automatically, because their root is in the spiritual dissatisfaction many are presently experiencing.

3

THE ORIGIN OF CREATION

Now that we have established that today there is a real need to study Kabbalah, it's time to learn some of the basics of this wisdom. Even though the scope of this book does not allow for a thorough study of the Upper Worlds, by the end of this chapter you will have a solid enough basis to continue, should you want to study Kabbalah in depth.

A word about drawings: Kabbalah books are, and always have been, filled with drawings. Drawings help describe spiritual states or structures. From the very beginning, Kabbalists have been using drawings as tools to explain what they experience along the spiritual path. Nevertheless, it is very important to remember that the drawings do *not* represent tangible objects. They are simply images used to explain *spiritual* states, which concern one's most intimate relationship with the Creator, with Nature.

THE SPIRITUAL WORLDS

Creation is made entirely of a desire to receive pleasure. This desire evolved in four phases, the last of which is called "a creature" (Figure 1). This template structure of evolution of desires is the basis for everything that exists.

Figure 1 describes the making of the creature. If we treat that making as a story, it will help us remember that the drawings describe emotional, spiritual states, not places or objects.

Before anything is created, it has to be thought out, planned. In this case, we are talking about Creation and the thought that caused Creation to happen. We call it "the Thought of Creation."

In the first chapter, we said that in the past, people's fear of Nature urged them to search for its plan for them and for all of us. In their observations, they discovered that Nature's plan is for us to receive pleasure. And not just any pleasure, like those we can feel in this world. Nature (which we've said is interchangeable with the term, "Creator") wants us to receive a very special kind of pleasure—the pleasure of becoming identical to Itself, to the Creator.

So if you look at Figure 1, you will see that the Thought of Creation is actually a desire to give pleasure (called "Light") to the creatures. This is also the root of Creation, where we all began.

Kabbalists use the term *Kli* (vessel, receptacle) to describe the desire to receive the pleasure, the Light. Now we can see why they called their wisdom, "the wisdom of Kabbalah" (the wisdom of receiving).

There is also a good reason why they called pleasure "Light." When the *Kli*—a creature, a person—feels the Creator, it is an experience of great wisdom that dawns on a person, as if something has dawned on me, and now I see the Light. When that happens to us, we realize that whatever wisdom has manifested, it has always been there, albeit hidden from the eye. It's as if the night's darkness has turned to daylight and the invisible has been made visible. And because this Light brings knowledge with it, Kabbalists called it "Light of Wisdom," and the method to receive it, "the wisdom of Kabbalah."

FOUR BASIC PHASES

Let's go back to our story. To put the thought of giving pleasure into practice, the Creator designed a Creation that specifically wants to receive the

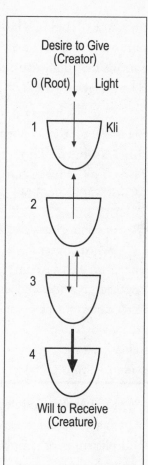

Figure 1: The five evolutionary phases of the will to receive. Downward arrows mark the Creator's entering Light; upward arrows mark the creature's desire to delight the Creator.

pleasure of being identical to the Creator. If you're a parent, you know how that feels. What warmer words can we say to a proud father than, "Your son's the spitting image of you!"?

As we've just said, the Thought of Creation—to give pleasure to the creature—is the root of Creation. For this reason, the Thought of Creation is called "the Root Phase" or "Phase Zero," and the desire to receive the pleasure is named "Phase One."

Note that Phase Zero is shown as a downward arrow. Whenever there's an arrow pointing down, it means that Light comes from the Creator to the creature. But the opposite is not true: whenever there's an upward arrow, it doesn't mean that the creature gives Light to the Creator, but that it wants to give back to Him. And what happens when there are two arrows pointing in opposite directions? Keep reading; you'll soon find out what this means.

Kabbalists also refer to the Creator as "the Will to Bestow," and to the creature as "the will to receive delight and pleasure" or simply "the will to receive." We will talk about our perception of the Creator later on, but what's important at this point is that Kabbalists always tell us what *they* perceive. They don't tell us that the Creator has a desire to give; they tell us that what they see of the Creator is that He has a desire to give, and this is why they called Him "the Will to Bestow." Because they also discovered in themselves a desire to receive the pleasure He wants to give, they called themselves, "the will to receive."

So the will to receive is the first Creation, the root of every single creature. When Creation, the will to receive, feels that the pleasure comes from a giver, it senses that real pleasure lies in giving, not in receiving. As a result, the will to receive begins to want to give (note the upward arrow extending from the second *Kli*—the cup in the drawing). This is a whole new phase—Phase Two.

Let's examine what makes this a new phase. If we look at the *Kli* itself, we see that it doesn't change throughout the phases. This means that the will to receive is just as active as it was before. Because the will to receive was designed in the Thought of Creation, it is eternal and can never be changed.

However, in Phase Two the will to receive wants to receive pleasure from *giving*, not from receiving, and this is a fundamental change. The great difference is that Phase Two needs another being to whom it can give. In other words, Phase Two has to relate positively to someone or something else besides itself.

Phase Two, which forces us to give despite our underlying desire to receive, is what makes life possible. Without it, parents wouldn't care for their children and social life would have been impossible. For example, if I own a restaurant, my desire is to make money, but the bottom line is that I am feeding strangers in whom I have no long-term interest. The same is true for bankers, cab drivers (even in New York), and everyone else.

Now we can see why Nature's law is altruism and giving, and not the law of receiving, even though the will to receive lies at the basis of every creature's motivation, just as in Phase One. From the minute Creation has both a desire to receive and a desire to give, everything that will happen to it will stem from the "relationship" between the first two phases.

As we've just shown, the desire to give in Phase Two forces it to communicate, to seek someone who needs to receive. Therefore, Phase Two now begins to examine what it can give to the Creator. After all, to whom else could it give?

But when Phase Two actually tries to give, it discovers that all the Creator wants is to give. He has absolutely no desire to receive. Besides, what can the creature give to the Creator?

Moreover, Phase Two discovers that at its core, in Phase One, its real desire is to receive. It discovers that its root is essentially a will to receive delight and pleasure, and there is not an ounce of genuine desire to bestow within it. But, and here lies the crux of the matter, because the Creator wants only to give, the creature's will to receive is precisely what it *can* give to the Creator.

This may sound confusing, but if you think of the pleasure a mother derives from feeding her baby, you will realize that the baby is actually giving pleasure to its mother simply by wanting to eat.

Therefore, in Phase Three, the will to receive *chooses* to receive, and in so doing gives back to Root Phase, to the Creator. Now we have a complete circle where both players are givers: Phase Zero, the Creator, gives to the creature, which is Phase One, and the creature, having gone through Phases One, Two, and Three, gives back to the Creator by receiving from Him.

In Figure 1, the downward arrow in Phase Three indicates that its act is reception, as in Phase One, but the upward arrow indicates that its *intention* is to give, as in Phase Two. And once again, both actions use the same will to receive as in Phases One and Two; this doesn't change at all.

As we've seen before, our egoistic intentions are the reason for all the problems we are seeing in the world. Here, too, at the root of Creation, the intention is much more important than the action itself. In fact, Yehuda Ashlag metaphorically says that Phase Three is ten percent a receiver and ninety percent a giver.

Now it seems we have a perfect cycle where the Creator has succeeded in making the creature identical to Himself—a giver. Moreover, the creature enjoys giving, thus returning pleasure to the Creator. But does this complete the Thought of Creation?

Not quite. The act of reception (in Phase One) and the understanding that the Creator's only wish is to give (in Phase Two) make the creature want to be in the same state, which is Phase Three. But becoming a giver doesn't mean that the creature will be in the same state, thus completing the Thought of Creation.

Being in the Creator's state means that the creature will not only become a giver, but will have the same *thought* as the Giver—the Thought of Creation. In such a state, the creature would understand why the Creator-creature circle was initiated, as well as why the Creator formed Creation.

Clearly, the desire to understand the Thought of Creation is a whole new phase. The only thing we can compare it to is a child who wants to be both as strong and as wise as its parents. We instinctively know that this is possible only when the child actually steps into his or her parents' shoes. This is why parents so often say to their kids, "Wait until you have children of your own; then you'll understand."

___

One of the most common terms in Kabbalah is *Sefirot*. The word comes from the Hebrew word, *Sapir* (sapphire) and each *Sefira* (singular for *Sefirot*) has its own Light. Also, each of the four phases is named after one or more *Sefira*. Phase Zero is named *Keter*, Phase One, *Hochma*, Phase Two, *Bina*, Phase Three, *Zeir Anpin*, and Phase Four, *Malchut*.

Actually, there are ten *Sefirot* because *Zeir Anpin* is composed of six *Sefirot*: *Hesed, Gevura, Tifferet, Netzah, Hod,* and *Yesod*. Therefore, the complete set of *Sefirot* is *Keter, Hochma, Bina, Hesed, Gevura, Tifferet, Netzah, Hod, Yesod,* and *Malchut*.

___

In Kabbalah, understanding the Thought of Creation—the deepest level of understanding—is called "attainment." This is what the will to receive craves in the last phase—Phase Four.

The desire to acquire the Thought of Creation is the most powerful force in Creation. It stands behind the whole process of evolution. Whether we are aware of it or not, the ultimate knowledge we all seek is the understanding of why the Creator does what He does. It is the same drive that urged Kabbalists to discover the secrets of Creation thousands of years ago. Until we understand it, we will have no peace of mind.

THE QUEST FOR THE THOUGHT OF CREATION

Even though the Creator wants us to receive the pleasure of becoming identical to Him, He didn't give us this desire to begin with. All that He gave us—the creature, the united soul of *Adam ha Rishon*—was a craving for the ultimate pleasure. However, as we can see in the sequence of phases, the Creator did not infuse the creature with a desire to be like Him; this is something that evolved within it through the phases.

In Phase Three, the creature had already received everything and intended to give back to the Creator. The sequence could have ended right then and there, as the creature was already doing exactly what the Creator was doing—giving. In that sense, they were now identical.

But the creature didn't settle for giving. It wanted to understand what makes giving pleasurable, why a giving force is necessary to create reality, and what wisdom the giver obtains by giving. In short, the creature wanted to understand the Thought of Creation. This was a new craving, one which the Creator did not "plant" in the creature.

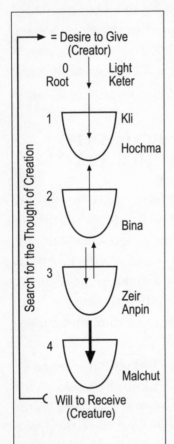

= Desire to Give (Creator)

0 Root   Light Keter

Search for the Thought of Creation

1   Kli   Hochma

2   Bina

3   Zeir Anpin

4   Malchut

Will to Receive (Creature)

Figure 2: The arrow from *Malchut* to the Creator indicates *Malchut's* focused desire on becoming Creator-like.

At this point in its quest for the Thought of Creation, the creature became a distinct, separated being from the Creator. We can look at it this way: If I want to be like someone else, it necessarily means that I'm aware that someone besides me exists, and that this someone has something that I want, or is something that I'd like to be.

In other words, I not only realize that there is someone else besides me, but I realize that that someone is different from me. And not just different, but better. Otherwise, why would I want to be like Him?

Therefore, *Malchut*, Phase Four, is very different from the first three phases because it wants to receive a very specific kind of pleasure (hence the thicker arrow)—that of being identical to the Creator. From the Creator's perspective, *Malchut's* desire completes the Thought of Creation, the cycle that He originally had in mind (Figure 2).

Regrettably, we're not looking at things from the Creator's perspective. Looking from down here, with our broken spiritual spectacles, the picture is less than ideal. For the *Kli* (a person), completely opposite from the Light, to become like the Light, it must use its will to receive with the *intention* to bestow. By doing that, it turns its focus from its own pleasure to the joy the Creator receives from giving. And in so doing, the *Kli*, too, becomes a giver.

Actually, receiving in order to give to the Creator already happened in Phase Three. With regard to the Creator's actions, Phase Three had already completed the job of becoming identical to the Creator. The Creator gives in order to bestow and Phase Three receives in order to bestow, so in that they are the same.

But the ultimate pleasure is not in knowing what the Creator does and replicating His actions. The ultimate pleasure is in knowing *why* He does what He does, and acquiring the same *thoughts* as His. And this, the highest part of Creation—the Creator's thought—has not been given to the creature; it is what the creature (Phase Four) must achieve.

There is a beautiful connection here. On the one hand, it seems as if the Creator and we are on opposite sides of the court, because He gives and we receive. But in fact, His greatest pleasure is for us to be like

Him, and our greatest pleasure would be to become like Him. Similarly, every child wants to become like its parents, and every parent naturally wants his or her kids to achieve even those things that the parent did not.

It turns out that we and the Creator are actually pursuing the same goal. If we could comprehend this concept, our lives would be very, very different. Instead of the confusion and disorientation so many of us experience today, both we and the Creator would be able to march together toward our designated goal since the dawn of Creation.

Kabbalists use many terms to describe the will to bestow: Creator, Light, Giver, Thought of Creation, Phase Zero, Root, Root Phase, *Keter*, *Bina*, and many others. Similarly, they use many terms to describe the will to receive: creature, *Kli*, receivers, Phase One, *Hochma*, and *Malchut* are just a few. These terms refer to subtleties in the two characteristics—bestowal and reception. If we remember that, we will not be confused by all the names.

To become like the Creator, a giver, the *Kli* does two things. First, it stops receiving, an act called *Tzimtzum* (restriction). It stops the Light entirely and doesn't allow any of it into the *Kli*. Similarly, it's easier to avoid eating something tasty, but unhealthy, than to eat just a little and leave the rest on the plate. Therefore, making a *Tzimtzum* is the first and easiest step to becoming like the Creator.

The next thing that *Malchut* does is to set up a mechanism that examines the Light (pleasure) and decides if it will receive it, and if so, how much. This mechanism is called *Masach* (screen). The condition by which the *Masach* determines how much to receive is called "aim to bestow" (Figure 3). In simple terms, the *Kli* only takes in what it can receive with the intention to please the Creator. The Light received within the *Kli* is called "Inner Light," and the Light that remains outside is called "Surrounding Light."

At the end of the correction process, the *Kli* will receive all of the Creator's Light and unite with Him. This is the purpose of Creation. When we reach that state, we will feel it both as individuals and as a single, united society, because in truth, the complete *Kli* is not made of one person's desires, but of the desires of the whole of humanity. And when we complete this last correction, we will become identical to the Creator, Phase Four will be fulfilled, and Creation will be completed from our perspective just as it is completed from His.

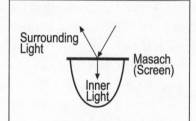

Figure 3: The *Masach* is the line that separates between the Light that the creature can receive with aim to bestow upon the Creator—Inner Light—and the Light it cannot receive with this aim—Surrounding Light.

THE ROUTE

To carry out the task of becoming identical to the Creator, the first thing the creature must obtain is the right environment to evolve and become Creator-like. This environment is called "worlds."

At Phase Four, the creature was divided into two parts: upper and lower. The upper part constitutes the worlds, and the lower part constitutes the creature, which is everything within these worlds. Roughly speaking, the worlds are made of desires where the *Masach* allowed the Light to enter Phase Four, and the creature will be made of desires where the *Masach* did not allow the Light to enter it.

We already know that Creation is made of one thing only: a will to receive delight and pleasure. Therefore, upper and lower do not relate to places, but to desires that *we* relate to as higher or lower. In other words, higher desires are desires we appreciate more than the desires we consider lower. In the case of Phase Four, any desire that can be used to bestow upon the Creator belongs in the upper part, and any desire that can't be used in this way belongs in the lower part.

Because there are five levels of desires—still, vegetative, animate, speaking, and spiritual—each level is analyzed. The workable ones create worlds, and the (as yet) unworkable ones create the creature.

Earlier in this chapter we said that the four-phase pattern is the basis for everything that exists. Therefore, the worlds evolve by the same model that worked in the creation of the phases. The left-hand side of Figure 4 is a look into the contents of Phase Four, showing its division into upper and lower parts, and that the upper part contains the worlds and the lower part contains the creature.

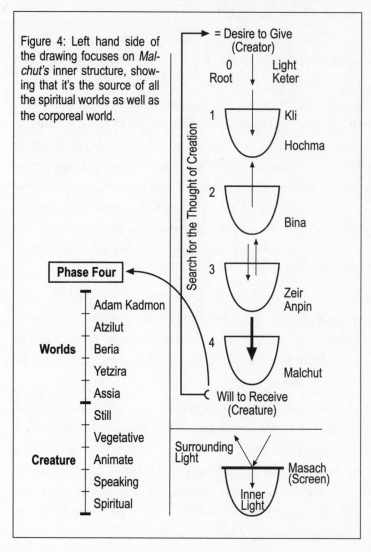

Figure 4: Left hand side of the drawing focuses on *Malchut's* inner structure, showing that it's the source of all the spiritual worlds as well as the corporeal world.

So let's talk some more about Phase Four and how it works with the *Masach*. After all, Phase Four is us, so if we understand how it works, we might learn something about ourselves.

Phase Four, *Malchut*, didn't just pop up out of nowhere. It evolved from Phase Three, which evolved from Phase Two, etc. Similarly, Abraham Lincoln didn't just pop up as president. He grew from baby Abe, to a child, to a youth, and to an adult who finally became president. But the preliminary phases don't disappear. Without them, President Lincoln would not have become President Lincoln. The reason we can't see them is because the most developed level always dominates and overshadows the less developed. But the last, highest level, not only feels their existence within it, it works with these other levels.

This is why there are times when we all feel like children, especially when touched in places where we haven't matured. It's simply that these places are not covered by a grownup layer, and those soft spots make us feel as defenseless as kids.

This multilayered structure is what enables us to eventually become parents. In the process of raising children, we combine our present and previous phases: we understand the situations our children experience because we'd had similar experiences. We relate to those situations with the knowledge and experience we've accumulated over the years.

The reason we are built this way is that *Malchut* (to call it by its commonly used name) is built in exactly the same way. All of *Malchut's* previous phases exist within it and help sustain its structure.

To become as similar to the Creator as possible, *Malchut* analyzes each level of desire within itself, and splits the desires into workable and unworkable ones within each level. But the workable desires will not only be used to receive in order to give to the Creator. They will also "help" the Creator complete His task of making *Malchut* identical to Him.

A few pages back, we said that to carry out the task of becoming identical to the Creator, the creature must create the right environment to evolve and become Creator-like. That's exactly what the worlds—workable desires—do. They "show" the unworkable desires how to receive in order to bestow upon the Creator, and in so doing, help the unworkable desires correct themselves.

We can picture the relationship between the worlds and the creature as a group of construction workers where one of the workers doesn't know what to do. The worlds teach the creature by demonstrating how to do each task: how to drill, how to use a hammer, a level, and so on. In the case of spirituality, the worlds show the creature what the Creator has given them and how they work with it in the right way. Bit by bit, the creature can begin to use its desires this way, too, which is why desires in our world surface gradually, from the mildest to the most intense.

Desires are divided in the following way: The world *Adam Kadmon* is the workable part of the still level, and the lower part of the still level, the creature, is the unworkable part. Actually, at the still level there is nothing to correct because it's immobile and doesn't use its desire. The still level (on both parts) is only the root of everything that will follow.

From all we've learned so far, we still don't know which of the five worlds we talked about is our world. Actually, none of them is ours. Keep in mind that there are no "places" in spirituality, only states. The higher the world, the more altruistic a state it represents. The reason our world is not mentioned anywhere is that the spiritual worlds are altruistic, and our world is, like us, egoistic. Because egoism is opposite to altruism, our world is detached from the system of the spiritual worlds. This is why Kabbalists did not mention it in the structure they depicted.

Moreover, the worlds don't actually exist unless we create them by becoming like the Creator. The reason they are spoken of in past tense is that Kabbalists who have climbed from our world to the spiritual worlds tell us what they've found. If we want to find the spiritual worlds as well, we will have to recreate these worlds within us by becoming altruistic.

Next, the world *Atzilut* is the workable part of the vegetative level, and the lower part of the vegetative level, the creature, is the unworkable part. The world *Beria* is the workable part of the animate level, and the lower part of the animate level, the creature, is the unworkable part.

The world *Yetzira* is the workable part of the speaking level, and the lower part of the speaking level, the creature, is the unworkable part. Finally, the world *Assiya* is the workable part of the spiritual, most intense level of desires, and the lower part of the spiritual level, the creature, is the unworkable part.

Now you know why, if we correct humanity, everything else will be corrected at the same time. So let's talk about us and what happened to us.

ADAM HA RISHON— THE COMMON SOUL

Adam ha Rishon, the common soul (the creature), is the actual root of everything that happens here. It is a structure of desires that emerged once the formation of the spiritual worlds was completed. As we've said above, the five worlds, *Adam Kadmon*, *Atzilut*, *Beria*, *Yetzira*, and *Assiya* complete the development of the upper part of Phase Four. But the lower part still needs to be developed.

In other words, the soul is made of unworkable desires that couldn't receive Light in order to give to the Creator when they were first created. Now they must surface one by one and become corrected—workable—with the help of the worlds, the workable desires.

Thus, just like the upper part of Phase Four, its lower part is divided into still, vegetative, animate, and speaking levels of desire. *Adam ha Rishon* evolves by the same degrees as the worlds and the four basic phases. But

Adam's desires are egoistic, self-centered; this is why he couldn't receive Light to begin with. As a result, we, the parts of Adam's soul, have lost the sensation of whole-ness and unity in which we were created.

We must understand how the spiritual system works. The Creator's desire is to give; this is why He created us and sustains us. As we've said, a desire to receive is self-centered by its nature; it absorbs, while a desire to give is necessarily focused outwardly towards the receiver. This is why a desire to receive cannot create. This is also why the Creator must have a desire to give, or He wouldn't be able to create.

However, because He wants to give, what He creates will necessarily want to receive, otherwise He will not be able to give. So He created us with a desire to receive, and with nothing else. This is important to understand; there is nothing within us other than a desire to receive, and there is nothing that *should* be in us other than a desire to receive. So if we receive from Him, the cycle is complete. He's happy and we're happy. Correct?

Actually, not quite. If all we want is to receive, then we can't relate to the giver because there's nothing in us that turns outwardly to see where the reception is coming from. It turns out that we must have a desire to receive, but we must also *know the giver*, and for that we need a desire to give. This is why we have Phase One *and* Phase Two.

The way to have both desires is not to create a new desire that was not instilled in us by the Creator. The way to do it is to look solely at the pleasure we are giving to the giver, regardless of the pleasure we may or may not experience in the process. This is called the "intention to bestow." It is both the essence of the correction, and what turns us as human beings from egoists to altruists. And finally, once we have acquired this quality, we can connect to the Creator, which is what the spiritual worlds are meant to teach us.

Until we feel connected to the Creator, we are considered broken pieces of the soul of *Adam ha Rishon*, uncorrected desires. The moment we have the intention to bestow, we become corrected and connected, both to the Creator and to the whole of humanity. When all of us are corrected, we will rise again to our Root Phase, even beyond the world *Adam Kadmon*, to the very Thought of Creation, called *Ein Sof* (No End), because our fulfillment will be endless and eternal.

IN A NUTSHELL

The Thought of Creation is to give delight and pleasure by making a creature that is similar to its maker. This Thought (Light) creates a will to receive delight and pleasure.

Subsequently, the will to receive begins to want to give because giving is more similar to the Creator, and that's clearly more desirable. The will to receive then decides to receive because that's the way to give pleasure to the Creator. After that, the will to receive wants to know the Thought that created it, because what greater pleasure could there be than to know everything? Finally, the will to receive (creature) begins to receive with the intention to bestow because giving makes it similar to the Creator, which is how it can study the Creator's thoughts.

Those desires that can receive in order to bestow create the worlds, which are considered the upper part of Creation, and desires that can't be used in order to bestow constitute the common soul of *Adam ha Rishon*. Those desires are considered the lower part of Creation.

The worlds and the soul are constructed similarly, but with a different intensity of desires. Because of that, the worlds can show the soul how to work in order to bestow and thus help *Adam ha Rishon* become corrected.

Roughly speaking, each desire is corrected in a specific world: the still level is corrected in the world *Adam Kadmon*; the vegetative in the world *Atzilut*; the animate in the world *Beria*; the speaking in the world *Yetzira*; and the desire for spirituality can only be corrected in the world *Assiya*, the lowest part of which is our physical universe. And that brings us to the topic of our next chapter.

4

OUR UNIVERSE

In the beginning of the previous chapter, we wrote that before anything was created, there was the Thought of Creation. This Thought created Phases One through Four of the will to receive, which created the worlds *Adam Kadmon* through *Assiya*, which then created the soul of *Adam ha Rishon*, which broke into the myriad souls we have today.

It's very important to remember this order of creation because it reminds us that things evolve from above downward, from spiritual to corporeal, and not the other way around. In practical terms, it means that our world is created and governed by the spiritual worlds.

Moreover, there is not a single event in our world that doesn't happen up there first. And the only difference between our world and the spiritual worlds is that events in the spiritual worlds reflect altruistic intentions, and events in our world reflect egoistic intentions.

Because of this cascading structure of the worlds, our world is called the "world of results" of spiritual processes and occurrences. Whatever we do here has no impact of any kind on the spiritual worlds. Therefore, if we want to change anything in our world, we have to first climb to the spiritual worlds, the "control room" of our world, and affect our world from there.

THE PYRAMID

Just as it happens in the spiritual worlds, everything in our world evolves along the same five stages from Zero to Four. Our world is built like a pyramid. At the bottom, the beginning of the evolution of this world, there is the still (inanimate) level, made of trillions of tons of matter (see Figure 5).

Lost in these trillions of tons of matter is a tiny speck called "Planet Earth." And on this Earth appeared the vegetative level. Naturally, the vegetation on Earth is infinitely smaller in mass than that of the still matter on Earth, all the more so compared to the quantity of matter in the whole universe.

The animate appeared after the vegetative, and has a tiny mass, even compared to the vegetative.

The speaking, of course, came last and has the least mass of all.

Recently, another level has sprung from the speaking level. It is called "the spiritual level" or "spirituality."

(Since we are speaking of geological times here, when we say recently, we mean that it happened only a few thousand years ago.) We cannot grasp the full size of Creation, but if we look at the pyramid of Creation (in Figure 5) and think of the proportions between each two neighboring levels, we will begin to understand just how special and recent the desire for spirituality really is. Actually, if we think of the time the universe has existed—approximately 15 billion years—as a single day of 24 hours, the desire for spirituality appeared 0.0288 seconds ago. In geological terms, this is now.

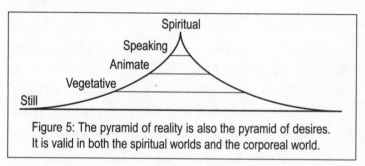

Figure 5: The pyramid of reality is also the pyramid of desires. It is valid in both the spiritual worlds and the corporeal world.

Thus, on the one hand, the higher the desire, the rarer (and younger) it is. On the other hand, the existence of a spiritual level, above the human level, indicates that we haven't completed our evolution. Evolution is as dynamic as ever, but because we are the last level to appear, we naturally think that we are the top level. We may be at the top level, but we are not at the final level. We are only at the last of the levels that have already appeared.

The final level will use our bodies as hosts, but will consist of entirely new ways of thinking, feeling and being. It is already evolving within us, and it is called "the spiritual level."

No physical changes or new species are required, just an inner change in our perception of the world. This is why the next phase is so elusive; it's within us, written in our *Reshimot* like data on a hard-drive. This data will be read and executed regardless of whether or not we are aware of it, but we can read and execute the data much more quickly and enjoyably if we read it with the right "software"—the wisdom of Kabbalah.

AS ABOVE, SO BELOW

If we draw a parallel between the earthly phases of the Four Basic Phases of Light, the still era corresponds to the Root Phase, the vegetative era corresponds to Phase One, the animate era to Phase Two, the speaking era to Phase Three, and the spiritual era to Phase Four.

Planet Earth's scorching youth lasted several billions of years. As it cooled, vegetative life appeared, reigning on the planet for many more millions of years. But just as the vegetative level on the spiritual pyramid is much narrower than the still level, the physical vegetative period was shorter than Earth's inanimate period.

After the completion of the vegetative phase came the animate period. As with the previous two degrees, the animate era was much shorter than the vegetative era, matching the proportion between the vegetative and the animate degrees on the spiritual pyramid.

The human phase, which corresponds to the speaking level of the spiritual pyramid, has only been around for the past forty thousand years or so. When humanity completes its evolution of the fourth (and last) phase, evolution will be complete and humanity will reunite with the Creator.

The Fourth Phase began some five thousand years ago, when the point in the heart first appeared. As in the spiritual world, the name of the man who first experienced this point was Adam. He was *Adam ha Rishon* (The First Man). The name, Adam, comes from the Hebrew words, *Adameh la Elyon* (I will be like the Upper One), and reflects Adam's desire to be like the Creator.

These days, at the start of the 21st century, evolution is completing its development of the Fourth Phase—the desire to be like the Creator. This is why today more and more people are looking for spiritual answers to their questions.

UP THE LADDER

When Kabbalists talk about spiritually evolving, they talk about climbing up the spiritual ladder. This is why Kabbalist Yehuda Ashlag named his commentary on *The Book of Zohar, Perush HaSulam* (*The Ladder Commentary*), for which he was named Baal HaSulam (Owner of the Ladder). But if we flip back a few pages, we'll find that "up the ladder" actually means "back to the roots." This is because we've already been up there, but now we have to figure out how to get back there by ourselves.

The root is our final goal; it is where we are ultimately heading. But to get there quickly and peacefully
we need a great desire for it—a *Kli*. Such a desire for spirituality can only come from the Light, from the Creator,
but to become strong enough, it needs to be intensified
by the environment.

Let's make it a little clearer: If I want a piece of cake,
I picture the cake in my mind, its texture, color, sweet
fragrance, and the way it melts in my mouth. The more
I think about it, the more I want it. In Kabbalah, we
would say that "the cake shines" for me with "Surrounding Light."

Therefore, to want spirituality, we need to acquire
the kind of Surrounding Light that will make us want
spiritual pleasures. The more of this Light we gather, the
faster we will progress. Wanting spirituality is called "raising MAN," and the technique for doing so is the same as
increasing the desire for a cake—picture it, talk about it,
read about it, think about it, and do whatever you can to
focus on it. But the most powerful means to increase any
desire is our social environment. We can use the environment to intensify our spiritual desire, our MAN, and
thus accelerate our progress.

We will talk about the environment more in Chapter Six, but for now, let's think of it this way: If everyone
around me wants and talks about the same thing, and
there's only one thing that's "in," I'm bound to want it.

In Chapter Two, we said that the appearance of a *Kli*, a desire, forces our brains to search for a way to fill this *Kli* with *Ohr* (Light), to satisfy it. The bigger the *Kli*, the greater the Light; the greater the Light, the quicker we'll find the correct path.

Is there a difference between naming the Light
"Surrounding Light" or just "Light"?

The different titles, "Surrounding Light" and "Light," relate to two functions of the same Light. Light that is *not* considered Surrounding is what we experience as pleasure, while Surrounding Light is the Light that builds our *Kli*, the place where the Light will finally enter. Both are actually one Light, but when we experience it as correcting and building we call it "Surrounding Light." When we feel it as pure pleasure, we call it "Light."

Before we develop a *Kli*, it is only natural that we will not receive any Light. But the Light is there, surrounding our souls just like Nature always surrounds us. So when we don't have a *Kli*, the Surrounding Light builds our *Kli* for us by increasing our desire for it.

We still need to understand how the Surrounding Light builds our *Kli* and why it is called "Light" to begin with. And to understand all that, we must understand the concept of *Reshimot*.

The spiritual worlds and the soul of *Adam ha Rishon* evolved in a certain order. In the worlds, it was *Adam Kadmon*, *Atzilut*, *Beria*, *Yetzira*, and *Assiya*; and in *Adam ha Rishon*, the evolution was named after the kind of desires that emerged—still, vegetative, animate, speaking, and spiritual.

Just as we don't forget our childhood, but rely on those past events in our present experiences, each completed step in the evolutionary process is not lost, but is registered in our unconscious "spiritual memory." In other words, within us lies the entire history of our spiritual evolution, from the time we were one with the Thought of Creation to this day. Going up the spiritual ladder simply means remembering the states we've already experienced once more, and uncovering those memories.

Those memories are aptly named *Reshimot* (records), and each *Reshimo* (singular for *Reshimot*) stands for a specific spiritual state. Because our spiritual evolution unfolded in a specific order, now the *Reshimot* surface within us in just that order. In other words, our future states are already determined because we're not creating anything new, just remembering events that already happened to us, of which we're unaware. The one thing we can determine, and we will discuss it at length in the following chapters, is how fast we can climb the ladder. The harder we work at climbing it, the faster these states will change and the faster our spiritual progress will be.

Each *Reshimo* is completed when we have fully experienced it, and like a chain, when one *Reshimo* ends, the next *Reshimo* emerges. This next *Reshimo* originally created the present *Reshimo*, but since now we're going back up the ladder, the present *Reshimo* is awakening its original creator. Thus, we should never expect to end our present state so we can rest, because when the present

state is over, it will lead to the next in line until we complete our correction.

When we try to become altruistic (spiritual) we come
closer to our corrected state because we awaken the *Reshimot* more quickly. And since those *Reshimot* are records
of higher spiritual experiences, the sensations they create
in us are more spiritual sensations.

When that happens, we begin to vaguely sense the
connectedness, unity, and love that exist in that state,
much like a distant, faint light. The more we try to reach
it, the closer we come to it, and the stronger it shines.
Moreover, the stronger the Light, the stronger our desire
for it, and thus the Light builds our *Kli*, our desire for
spirituality.

Now we also see that the name, "Surrounding Light,"
perfectly describes how we sense it. As long as we haven't
reached it, we see it as external, attracting us with its
blinding promise of bliss.

Every time the Light builds a big enough *Kli* for us
to step to the next level, the next *Reshimo* comes along
and a new desire emerges in us. We don't know why our
desires change, because they're always parts of *Reshimot*
from a higher degree than our current level, even when
they don't seem like it.

So just like the last *Reshimo* surfaced, bringing us to
our present state, a new desire now approaches from a
new *Reshimo*. This is how we continue our climb up the
ladder. It is a spiral of *Reshimot* and ascents that end at
the purpose of Creation—the root of our souls, when
we're equal and united with the Creator.

THE DESIRE
FOR SPIRITUALITY

Different Strokes for Different Folks

The only difference between people is in the way they want to experience pleasure. The pleasure in itself, however, is amorphous, intangible. But covering it with different "dresses," or "coatings," creates an illusion that there are different kinds of pleasure, when in fact there are many different kinds of coatings.

The fact that pleasure is essentially spiritual explains why we have an unconscious craving to replace the superficial coating of the pleasure with the desire to feel it in its pure, unadulterated form: the Creator's Light.

And because we're unaware that the difference between people is in the coatings of pleasure they wish for, we judge them according to the coatings they prefer. We consider certain coatings of pleasure legitimate, such as love of children, while others, such as drugs, are considered unacceptable. When we feel an unacceptable coating for pleasure emerging in us, we are forced to conceal our desire for that coating. However, concealing a desire doesn't make it go away, and certainly doesn't correct it.

As we've explained in the previous section, the lower part of Phase Four is the substance of the soul of *Adam ha Rishon*. Just as the worlds are built according to the growing desires, Adam's soul (humanity) evolved through five phases: Zero (still) through Four (spiritual).

When each phase arises, humanity experiences it to the fullest until it exhausts itself. Then, the next level of desire surfaces, according to the sequence of *Reshimot* embedded in us. Until today, we had already experienced all the *Reshimot* of all the desires from still to speaking. All that's left for the evolution of humanity to be complete is for us to experience the spiritual desires to the fullest. Then, our unity with the Creator will be achieved.

Actually, the appearance of desires at the fifth level began back in the 16th century, as was described by Kabbalist Isaac Luria (the Ari), but today we are witnessing the appearance of the most intense kind within the fifth level—the spiritual within the spiritual. Moreover, we are witnessing its appearance in huge numbers, when millions of people the world over are seeking spiritual answers to their questions.

Because the *Reshimot* that surface today are closer to spirituality than they previously were, the primary questions people are asking are about their origins, their roots! Although most of them have a roof over their heads and earn enough to support themselves and their families, they have questions about where they came from, by whose plan, and for what purpose. When they are not satisfied with the answers religions offer, they seek them from other disciplines.

The main difference between Phase Four and all other phases is that in this phase, we must *consciously* evolve. In previous phases, it was always Nature that compelled us to move from phase to phase. It did this by pressuring us enough to feel so uncomfortable in our present state that we had to change it. This is how

Nature develops all of its parts: human, animate, vegetative, and even inanimate.

Because we are naturally lazy, we will only move from one state to the next when the pressure becomes intolerable. Otherwise, we wouldn't lift a finger. The logic is simple: If I'm fine where I am, why move?

But Nature has a different plan. Instead of allowing us to remain complacent in our present state, it wants us to evolve until we reach its own level, the level of the Creator. This is the purpose of Creation.

So we have two options: we could choose to evolve through Nature's (painful) pressure, or we can evolve painlessly by participating in the development of our awareness. Remaining undeveloped is not an option, as it doesn't fit into Nature's plan when it created us.

When our spiritual level begins to evolve, it can only happen if we *want* it to evolve and to reach the same condition as the Creator's. Just like Phase Four in the Four Phases, we are now required to *voluntarily* change our desire.

Therefore, Nature will continue pressuring us. We will continue to be struck by hurricanes, earthquakes, epidemics, terrorism, and all kinds of natural and manmade adversities until we realize that we *have* to change, that we must consciously return to our Root.

Just to review: our spiritual root evolved along Phases Zero through Four; Phase Four split into worlds (its upper part) and souls (its lower part). The souls—collected in the common soul of *Adam ha Rishon*—broke off by losing their sense of oneness with the Creator. This breaking of Adam ha Rishon brought humanity to its present state, with an unseen barrier that separates the spiritual worlds (above it) from our world (below).

Below the barrier, the spiritual force created a corporeal particle, which began to evolve. This was the Big Bang.

Keep in mind that when Kabbalists talk about the spiritual world and the corporeal, physical world, they are referring to altruistic or egoistic features, respectively. They *never* refer to worlds that take up physical space in some undiscovered universe.

We can't take a spaceship and fly to the world *Yetzira*, for example, or even discover spirituality by changing our behavior. We can only discover it by becoming altruistic—similar to the Creator. When we do that, we will discover that the Creator is already within us and that He has always been here, waiting for us.

All degrees prior to the last, evolve without awareness of their "selves." In terms of our personal awareness, the fact that we exist doesn't mean that we are *aware* of our existence. Before we reach the fourth level, we merely exist. In other words, we live our lives as comfortably as we can, but we take our existence for granted without asking about its purpose.

But is it really that obvious? Minerals exist so that plants can feed on them and grow; plants exist so animals can feed on them and grow; minerals, plants, and animals exist so humans can feed on them and grow. But what is the purpose of human existence? All the levels serve us, but what or whom do we serve? Ourselves? Our egos? When we first ask these questions, it is the beginning of our conscious evolution, the emergence of the desire for spirituality. This is called the "point in the heart."

In the last evolutionary degree, we begin to understand the process we are parts of. Simply put, we begin to acquire Nature's logic. The more we understand its logic, the more we expand our consciousness and integrate with it. In the end, when we have fully mastered Nature's logic, we will understand how Nature works and even learn to master it. This process occurs exclusively at the last level, the level of spiritual ascent.

We must always remember that our final level of human development should unfold consciously and willingly. Without an explicit desire for spiritual growth, no spiritual evolution can occur. After all, the spiritual evolution from above downward had already happened. We have been brought down the Four Phases of Light to the five worlds *Adam Kadmon, Atzilut, Beria, Yetzira,* and *Assiya,* and were finally placed here in this world.

If we are now to climb back up the spiritual ladder, we must *choose* to do so. If we forget that the purpose of Creation is for us to become like the Creator, we will not understand why Nature doesn't help us—and sometimes even places obstacles on our way.

But if, on the other hand, we keep only Nature's goal in mind, we will feel that our lives are a fascinating voyage of discovery, a spiritual treasure hunt. Moreover, the more actively we participate in this *Tour-de-Life*, the faster and easier these discoveries will come. Better yet, the hardships will be felt as questions we must answer, instead of ordeals we must face in our physical lives. This is why evolving by our own awareness is so much better than evolving only after Nature gives us a painful push from behind!

If we have a desire to evolve in spirituality, then we have the right *Kli* for it, and there is no better feeling than a filled *Kli*, a fulfilled desire.

But the desire for spirituality must come before the spiritual filling. Preparing the *Kli* before the Light is not only the sole means of ascending in the fourth phase; it is also the only means in which no pain and shortage is involved.

In fact, if we think about it, there is nothing more natural than to prepare the *Kli* first. If I want to drink water, then water is my light, my pleasure. Naturally, to drink water I must prepare the (*Kli*) first, which in this case will be thirst. And the same applies for anything we want to receive in this world. If a new car is my light, then my desire for it is my *Kli*. This *Kli* makes me work for the car, and ensures that I don't squander my money on other whims.

The only difference between a spiritual *Kli* and a physical one is that I don't quite know what I will receive with a spiritual *Kli*. I may imagine it as all kinds of things, but because there is a barrier between my present state and my desired goal, I can never really know what my goal will be like until I actually reach it. When I do reach it, it is greater than anything I could ever imagine; but I'll never know for sure how great it is until I have actually reached it. If I knew my reward in advance, it wouldn't be real altruism, but disguised egoism.

IN A NUTSHELL

The physical world evolves by the same order of degrees as the spiritual world, through a pyramid of desires. In the spiritual world, the desires (still, vegetative, animate, speaking, and spiritual) create the worlds *Adam Kadmon*, *Atzilut*, *Beria*, *Yetzira*, and *Assiya*. In the physical world, they create minerals, plants, animals, people, and people with "points in their hearts."

The physical world was created when the soul of *Adam ha Rishon* shattered. In that state, all the desires began to appear one by one from light to heavy, from still to spiritual, creating our world phase by phase.

Today, at the beginning of the 21st century, all the degrees have already been completed except for the desire for spirituality, which is surfacing now. When we correct it, we will unite with the Creator because our desire for spirituality is actually the desire for unity with the Creator. This will be the climax of the evolutionary process of the world and of humanity.

By increasing our desire to return to our spiritual root, we build a spiritual *Kli*. The Surrounding Light cor-

rects the *Kli* and develops it. Each new level of development evokes a new *Reshimo*, a record of a past state that
we had already experienced when we were more corrected. Eventually, the Surrounding Light corrects the whole
Kli, and the soul of *Adam ha Rishon* is reunited with all its
parts and with the Creator.

But this process leads to a question: if the *Reshimot*
are recorded within me, and if the states are evoked and
experienced within me, too, then where is the objective
reality in all of this? If another person has different *Reshimot*, does that mean that he or she is living in a different
world than mine? And what about the spiritual worlds,
where do they exist, if everything exists within me? Moreover, where is the Creator's home? Keep reading, the next
chapter will answer all these questions.

5

WHOSE REALITY IS REALITY?

All the worlds, upper and lower,
are contained within.

—Yehuda Ashlag

Of all the unexpected concepts found in Kabbalah, there is none so unpredictable, unreasonable, yet so profound and fascinating as the concept of reality. Had it not been for Einstein and Quantum Physics, which revolutionized the way we think about reality, the ideas presented here would have been brushed off and ridiculed.

In the previous chapter, we said that evolution occurs because our will to receive pleasure progresses from the Root level to the Fourth. But if our desires propelled the evolution of our world, then does the world actually exist outside of us? Could it be that the world around us is really just a tale we *want* to believe?

We've said that Creation started from the Thought of Creation, which created the Four Basic Phases of Light. These Phases include ten *Sefirot*: *Keter* (Phase Zero), *Hochma* (Phase One), *Bina* (Phase Two), *Hesed, Gevura, Tifferet, Netzah, Hod,* and *Yesod* (all of which comprise Phase Three—*Zeir Anpin*), and *Malchut* (Phase Four).

The Book of Zohar, the book that every Kabbalist studies, says that all of reality consists of only ten *Sefirot*. Everything is made of structures of these ten *Sefirot*. The only difference between them is how deeply they are immersed in our substance—the will to receive.

To understand what Kabbalists mean when they say that "they are immersed in our substance," think of a shape, say a ball, pressed into a piece of plasticine or another kind of modeling clay. The shape represents a group of ten *Sefirot*, and the clay represents us, or our souls. Now, even if you press the ball deep into the clay, the ball itself will not change. But the deeper the ball is immersed in the clay, the more it changes the clay.

How does that feel when the players are a group of ten *Sefirot* and a soul? Have you ever suddenly noticed something that was always around you, but a certain feature of it slipped your attention? This is similar to the sensation of the ten *Sefirot* sinking just a little deeper into the will to receive. In simple words, when we suddenly realize something we hadn't realized before, it's because the ten *Sefirot* went a little deeper into us.

Kabbalists have a name for the will to receive—*Aviut*. *Aviut* actually means thickness, not desire. But they use this term because the greater the will to receive, the more layers are added to it.

As we've said, the will to receive, the *Aviut*, consists of five basic degrees—0, 1, 2, 3, 4. As the ten *Sefirot* immerse deeper into the levels (layers) of *Aviut*, they form a variety of combinations, or mixtures of the will to receive with the desire to give. These combinations make up everything that exists: the spiritual worlds, the corporeal world, and everything within them.

The variations in our substance (will to receive) create our tools of perception, called *Kelim* (plural for *Kli*). In other words, every shape, color, scent, thought—everything that exists—is there because within me there is an appropriate *Kli* to perceive it.

Just as our brains use the letters of the alphabet to study what this world has to offer, our *Kelim* use the ten *Sefirot* to study what the spiritual worlds offer. And just as we study this world under certain restrictions and rules, to study the spiritual worlds we need to know the rules that shape those worlds.

When we study something in the physical world, we must follow certain rules. For example, for something to be considered true, it must be empirically tested. If tests show that it works, it's considered correct, until someone shows—in tests, not in words—that it doesn't work. Before something is tested, it's nothing but a theory.

The spiritual worlds have boundaries, too—three of them, to be exact. If we are to reach the purpose of Creation and become like the Creator, we must stick to these boundaries.

THREE BOUNDARIES IN LEARNING KABBALAH

FIRST BOUNDARY—WHAT WE PERCEIVE

In his *Preface to The Book of Zohar*, Kabbalist Yehuda Ashlag writes that there are "four categories of perception—Matter, Form in Matter, Abstract Form, and Essence." When we examine the spiritual Nature, it is our job to decide which of these categories provide us with solid, reliable information, and which do not.

The *Zohar* chose to explain only the first two. In other words, every single word in it is written either from the perspective of Matter or Form in Matter, with not a single word from the perspectives of Abstract Form or Essence.

SECOND BOUNDARY—WHERE WE PERCEIVE

As we've said before, the substance of the spiritual worlds is called "the soul of *Adam ha Rishon*." This is how the spiritual worlds were created. However, we have already passed the creation of these worlds, and are on our way up to higher levels, though it doesn't always feel like it.

In our state, Adam's soul has already broken in pieces. *The Zohar* teaches that the vast majority of the pieces,

99 percent to be exact, were scattered to the worlds *Beria*, *Yetzira*, and *Assiya* (BYA), and the remaining one percent rose to *Atzilut*.

Since Adam's soul makes up the content of the worlds *BYA* and has been scattered throughout these worlds, and since we are all pieces of that soul, clearly everything we perceive can only be parts of these worlds. Everything we sense as coming from higher worlds than BYA, such as *Atzilut* and *Adam Kadmon*, is therefore inaccurate, whether or not it appears that way to us. All we can perceive of the worlds *Atzilut* and *Adam Kadmon* are their reflections, as seen through the filters of the worlds *BYA*.

Our world is at the lowest degree of the worlds *BYA*. In fact, this degree is completely opposite in Nature from the rest of the spiritual worlds, which is why we don't feel them. It is as if two people are standing back to back and going in opposite directions. What are their chances of ever meeting each other?

But when we correct ourselves, we discover that we are already living inside the worlds *BYA*. Eventually, we will even rise along with them to *Atzilut* and to *Adam Kadmon*.

THIRD BOUNDARY—WHO PERCEIVES

Even though *The Zohar* goes into great detail about the content of each world and what happens there, as if there is a physical place where these things occur, it is actually referring only to the experiences of souls. In other words, it relates to how Kabbalists *perceive* things, and tells us so that we, too, can experience them. Therefore, when we are reading in *The Zohar* about events in the worlds BYA, we are actually learning about how Rabbi Shimon Bar-Yochai (author of *The Book of Zohar*) perceived spiritual states, as told by his son, Rabbi Abba.

Also, when Kabbalists write about the worlds above BYA, they are not actually writing about those worlds specifically, but about how *the writers* perceived those worlds while being in the worlds BYA. And because Kabbalists write about their personal experiences, there are similarities and differences in Kabbalistic writings. Some of what they write relates to the general structure of the worlds, such as the names of the *Sefirot* and the worlds. Other things relate to personal experiences that they experience in these worlds.

For example, if I tell a friend about my trip to New York, I might talk about Times Square or the great bridges that connect Manhattan to the mainland. But I might also talk about how overwhelmed I felt driving through the massive Brooklyn Bridge, and what it feels like to stand in the middle of Times Square, engulfed in the dazzling display of light, color, and sound, and the sense of total anonymity. The difference between the first two examples and the latter two is that in the latter pair I am reporting personal experiences, and in the first two, I am speaking of impressions that everyone will experience while in Manhattan, though everyone will experience them differently.

When we talked about the First Boundary, we said that *The Zohar* speaks only from the perspectives of Matter and Form in Matter. *The Zohar* also explains that Matter is the will to receive, and Form in Matter is the intention for which the will to receive actually receives—for me or for others. In simpler terms: Matter = will to receive; Form = intention.

It is imperative to remember that *The Zohar* shouldn't be treated like a report of mystical events or a collection of tales. *The Zohar*, like all other Kabbalah books, should be used as a learning tool. This means that the book will help you only if you, too, want to experience what it describes. Otherwise, the book will be of little help to you, and you will not understand it.

Remember this: Understanding Kabbalistic texts correctly depends on your *intention* while reading them, on the reason why you opened them, *not* on the power of your intellect. Only if you want to be transformed into the altruistic qualities that the text describes will the text affect you.

The Form of bestowal in and of itself is called "the world *Atzilut*." Bestowal in its Abstract Form is the attribute of the Creator; it is totally unrelated to the creatures, who are receivers by their nature. However, the creatures (people) *can* wrap their will to receive with the *Form* of bestowal, so it *resembles* bestowal. In other words, we can receive, and in so doing actually become givers.

There are two reasons why we cannot simply give:

1. To give, there must be someone who wants to receive. However, besides us (the souls), there is only the Creator, who has no need to receive anything, since His nature is to give. Therefore, giving is not a viable option for us.

2. We have no desire for it. We cannot give because we are made of a will to receive; reception is our substance, our Matter.

Now, this latter reason is more complex than it may seem at first. When Kabbalists write that all we want is to receive, they don't mean that all we *do* is receive, but that this is the underlying motivation behind everything we do. They phrase it very plainly: If it doesn't give us pleasure, we can't do it. It's not only that we don't want to; we literally can't. This is because the Creator (Nature) created us with only a will to receive, because all He wants is to give. Therefore, we need not change our actions, but only the underlying motivation behind them.

PERCEPTION OF REALITY

Many terms are used to describe understanding. For Kabbalists, the deepest level of understanding is called "attainment." Since they are studying the spiritual worlds, their goal is to reach "spiritual attainment." Attainment refers to such profound and thorough understanding of the perceived that no questions remain. Kabbalists write that at the end of humanity's evolution, we will all attain the Creator in a state called "Equivalence of Form."

To reach that goal, Kabbalists carefully defined which parts of reality we should study, and which we shouldn't. To determine these two paths, Kabbalists followed a very simple principle: If it helps us learn more quickly and more accurately, we should study it. If it doesn't, we should ignore it.

Kabbalists in general, and *The Zohar* in particular, caution us to study only those parts we can perceive with absolute certainty. Wherever guesswork is involved, we shouldn't waste our time, as our attainment would be questionable.

Kabbalists also say that of the four categories of perception—Matter, Form in Matter, Abstract Form, and Essence—we can perceive only the first two with certainty. For this reason, everything *The Zohar* writes about is desires (Matter) and how we use them: whether for ourselves or for the Creator.

Kabbalist Yehuda Ashlag writes that, "If the reader does not know how to be prudent with the boundaries, and takes matters out of context, he or she will immediately be confused." This can happen if we don't limit our study to Matter and Form in Matter.

We must understand that there is no such thing as a "prohibition" in spirituality. When Kabbalists declare something as "forbidden," it means that it is impossible. When they say that we shouldn't study Abstract Form and Essence, it doesn't mean that we'll be struck by lightning if we do; it means that we can't study those categories even if we really want to.

Yehuda Ashlag uses electricity to explain why the Essence is imperceptible. He says that we can use electricity in many different ways: for heating, cooling, playing music, and watching videos. Electricity can be dressed in many Forms; but can we express the Essence of electricity itself?

Let's use another example to explain the four categories—Matter, Form in Matter, Abstract Form, and Essence. When we say that a certain person is strong, we are actually referring to that person's Matter—body—and the Form that clothes his or her Matter—strength.

If we remove the Form of strength from the Matter (the person's body), and examine the Form of strength separately, undressed in Matter, this would be examining the Abstract Form of strength. The fourth category, the Essence of the person in itself, is completely unattainable. We simply have no senses that can "study" the Essence and portray it in a perceptible form. In consequence, the Essence is not only something we don't know right now; we will *never* know it.

Why is it so important to focus on just the first two categories? The problem is that when dealing with spirituality, we don't know when we are confused. Therefore, we continue in the same direction and drift farther away from the truth.

In the material world, if I know what I want, I can see if I am getting it or not, or at least if I'm on the right track toward getting it. This is not the case with spirituality. There, when I am wrong, I am not only denied what I wanted, but I even lose my present spiritual degree, the

Light dims, and I become unable to redirect myself correctly without help from a guide. This is why it is so important to understand the three boundaries and follow them.

A NONEXISTENT REALITY

Now that we understand what we can study and what we can't, let's see what we are actually studying through our senses. The thing about Kabbalists is that they leave no stone unturned. Yehuda Ashlag, who researched the whole of reality so he could tell us about it, wrote that we do not know what exists outside ourselves. For example, we have no idea what is outside our ears, what makes our eardrums respond. All we know is our own reaction to a stimulus from the outside.

Even the names we attach to phenomena are not connected to the phenomena themselves, but to our reactions to them. Most likely, we are unaware of many things that happen in the world. They can go unnoticed by our senses because we relate only to phenomena we can perceive. For that reason, it is quite obvious why we can't perceive the Essence of anything outside of us; we can only study our own reactions to it.

This rule of perception applies not only to the spiritual worlds; it's the law of all Nature. Relating to reality in this way immediately makes us realize that what we see is not what actually exists. This understanding is paramount to achieving spiritual progress.

When we observe our reality, we begin to discover things we were never aware of. We interpret things that occur within us as if they were happening on the outside. We don't know the actual sources of the events we experience, but we *feel* they are happening outside us. However, we can never know this for sure.

To relate correctly to reality, we mustn't think that what we are perceiving is the "real" picture. All we are perceiving is how events (Forms) affect our perception (our Matter). Moreover, what we perceive is not the outside, objective picture, but our own reaction to it. We cannot even say if and to what extent the Forms we sense are connected to the Abstract Forms we attach them to. In other words, the fact that we see a red apple as red doesn't mean that it is actually red.

Actually, if you ask physicists, they'll tell you that the only true statement you can make about a red apple is that it's *not* red. If you remember how the *Masach* (Screen) works, you know that it receives what it can receive in order to give to the Creator and rejects the rest.

Similarly, an object's color is determined by light waves that the illuminated object *could not* absorb. We are not seeing the color of the object itself, but the light that the object *rejected*. The real color of the object is the light that it absorbed; but because it absorbed this light, it cannot reach our eye, and we therefore can't see it. This is why the red apple's real color is anything but red.

Here's how Ashlag, in the *Preface to The Book of Zohar*, relates to our lack of perception of the Essence: "It is known that what we cannot feel, we also cannot imagine; and what we cannot sense, we cannot imagine, either. ...

It follows that the thought has no perception of the Essence whatsoever."

In other words, because we cannot sense an Essence, any Essence, we also cannot perceive it. But the concept that leaves most Kabbalah students completely baffled the first time they study Ashlag's Preface is how little we really know about ourselves. Here's what Ashlag writes concerning this: "Moreover, we do not even know our own Essence. I feel and know that I occupy a certain space in the world, that I am solid, warm, and that I think, and other such manifestations of the operations of my Essence. Yet, if you ask me what is my own Essence ... I will not know what to answer you."

THE MEASUREMENT MECHANISM

Let's look at our perception problem from another angle, a more mechanical one. Our senses are measurement instruments. They measure everything that they perceive. When we hear a sound, we determine if it's loud or soft; when we see an object, we can (usually) tell which color it is; and when we touch something, we immediately know if it's warm or cool, wet or dry.

All measurement tools operate similarly. Think of a scale with a one-kilogram weight on it. The traditional weighing mechanism is made of a spring that stretches according to the weight, and a ruler that measures the tightness of the spring. Once the spring stops stretching and rests at a certain point, the numbers on the ruler indicate the weight. Actually, we do not measure the weight, but

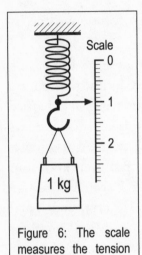

Figure 6: The scale measures the tension in the spring, not the weight itself.

the balance between the spring and the weight (Figure 6).

This is why Kabbalist Ashlag says that we cannot perceive the Abstract Form, the object in and of itself, because we have absolutely no connection with it. If we can place a spring on it to measure the external impact, we'll get some result. But if we can't measure what is happening on the outside, it's as though nothing is happening. Moreover, if we place a defective spring to measure an external stimulus, we will get the wrong result. This is what happens when we grow old and our senses deteriorate.

In spiritual terms, the outside world presents Abstract Forms to us, such as the weight. Using the spring and the dial—the will to receive and the intention to bestow—we measure how much of the Abstract Form we can receive. If we could build a gauge that would "measure" the Creator, we could feel Him just as we feel this world. Well, there is such a gauge; it is called "the sixth sense."

THE SIXTH SENSE

Let's begin this section with a little fantasy: We are in a dark space, a complete void. We cannot see a thing, we cannot hear a sound, there are no smells and no flavors, and there is nothing we can touch around us. Now imagine being in this state for such a long time that you forget you ever had senses that could feel such things. Eventually, you even forget that such sensations could exist.

All of a sudden, a faint aroma appears. It strengthens and engulfs you, but you can't pinpoint its source. Then, more fragrances appear, some strong, some weak, some sweet, and some sour. Using them, you can now find your way in the world. Different aromas come from different places, and you can begin to find your way by following them.

Then, without forewarning, sounds appear from all directions. The sounds are all different, some like music, some like words, and some just noises. But the sounds provide additional orientation in that space.

Now you can measure distances, directions; you can guess the sources of the smells and the sounds you are receiving. This is no longer just a space you're in; it's a whole world of sounds and scents.

After some time, a new revelation is made when something touches you. Shortly after, you discover more things you can touch. Some are cold, some are warm, some are dry, and some are moist. Some are hard and some are soft; some you can't decide which they are. You discover that you can put some of the objects you are touching in your mouth, and that they have distinct flavors.

By now you are living in a plentiful world of sounds, smells, sensations, and flavors. You can touch the objects in your world, and you can study your environment.

This is the world of the blind-from-birth. If you were in their shoes, would you feel that you needed the sense of sight? Would you even know that you don't have it? Never. Unless you'd had it before.

The same is true for the sixth sense. We don't remember ever having it, although we'd all had it prior to the breaking of *Adam ha Rishon*, of which we are all parts.

The sixth sense operates much like the five natural senses, with the only difference being that the sixth sense is not given by nature, we have to develop it. In fact, the name "sixth sense" is a bit misleading, because we are not actually developing another sense; we are developing an *intention*.

While developing this intention, we study the Creator's Forms, the Forms of bestowal, opposite from our natural egoistic makeup. This is why the sixth sense is not given to us by Nature; it is opposite from us.

Building the intention over each desire we feel is what makes us conscious of who we are, who the Creator is, and whether or not we want to be like Him. Only if we have two options before us can we make a real choice. Therefore, the Creator does not force us to be like Him—altruistic—but shows us who we are, who He is, and gives us the opportunity to make our own free choice. Once we've made our choice, we become the people we intend to be: Creator-like, or not.

Why, then, do we call the intention to bestow "the sixth sense"? Because by having the same intention as the

Creator, we become Creator-like. This means that we not only have the same intention, but because we have developed equivalence of form with Him, we see and perceive things we would not and could not perceive otherwise. We actually begin to see through His eyes.

WHERE THERE'S A WAY, THERE WAS A WILL

Back in the first chapter, we said that the concept of the *Kli* (tool/vessel) and *Ohr* (Light) is unquestionably the most important concept in the wisdom of Kabbalah. Actually, of the *Kli* and *Ohr*, the first is more important to us, even though obtaining the second is the actual goal.

Let's clarify this with an example. In the film, *What the Bleep Do We Know!?*, Dr. Candace Pert explains that if a certain Form does not exist within me in advance, I will not be able to see it on the outside. As an example, she uses a story about Indians who stood on the ocean shore and looked at Columbus's armada arriving. She says that it is commonly believed that the Indians could not see the ships, even though they were looking straight at them.

Dr. Pert explained that the Indians couldn't see the ships because they didn't have a similar preexisting model of ships in their minds. Only the shaman, who was curious about the odd ripples that seemed to come from nowhere, discovered the ships after trying to imagine what could be causing the ripples. When he discovered the ships, he told his tribesmen, described what he saw, and then they, too, could see the ships.

Kabbalistically speaking, it takes an inner *Kli* to detect an outer object. In fact, the *Kelim* (plural for *Kli*) not only detect the outer reality, they create it! Thus, Columbus' armada existed only in the minds, the inner *Kelim* of the Indians who saw it and reported it.

If a tree falls in a forest, and nobody is around to hear it, does it still make a sound?

This famous Zen *koan* (a special kind of Zen riddle) can also be phrased in Kabbalistic terms: If there is no *Kli* that detects the sound of the tree, how can we know that it made a sound at all?

Similarly, we could turn Columbus' discovery into a Zen *koan* and ask, "Before Columbus discovered America, did it exist?"

There is no such thing as an outside world. There are desires, *Kelim* that create the outside world according to their own shapes. Outside us there is only Abstract Form, the intangible, imperceptible Creator. We shape our world through shaping our own tools of perception, our own *Kelim*.

For this reason, it will not help if we pray to the Creator to help us out of our miseries or to change the world around us for the better. The world is neither good nor bad; it's a reflection of the state of our own *Kelim*. When we correct our *Kelim* and make them beautiful, the world will be beautiful, as well. The *Tikkun* is within, and so is the Creator. He is our corrected selves.

Similarly, to a night owl, a night in the dark forest is the time of best visibility. To us, it is a time of chilling blindness. Our reality is but a projection of our inner *Kelim*. And what we call "the real world" is but a reflection of our inner correction or corruption. We're living in an imaginary world.

If we are to rise above this imaginary world to the real world, to the true perception, we must adapt ourselves to the true models. At the end of the day, whatever we perceive will be according to our inner makeup, according to the way we build these models within us. There is nothing to discover outside of us, nothing to reveal except the abstract Upper Light that operates on us and reveals the new images within us, according to our readiness.

Now all that remains is to find out where we can find the corrected *Kelim*. Do they exist within us or do we have to build them? And if we have to build them, how do we go about it? This will be the topic of the following sections.

THE THOUGHT OF CREATION

Kelim are the building blocks of the soul. The desires are the building materials, the bricks and the wood; and our intentions are our tools, our screwdrivers, drills, and hammers.

But as with building a house, we need to read the blueprint before we can begin the work. Unfortunately, the Creator, the Architect of the blueprint, is reluctant to give it to us. Instead, he wants us to study and execute the

Master Plan of our souls independently. Only in this way can we ever really understand His Thought and become like Him.

To learn who He is, we must attentively watch what He does and learn to understand Him through His actions. Kabbalists phrase it very concisely: "By Your actions, we know You."

Our desires, the souls' raw materials, already exist. He gave them to us, and we just have to learn how to use them correctly and place the right intentions over them. Then, our souls will be corrected.

But as we have said before, the right intentions are altruistic intentions. In other words, we need to want for our desires to be used to benefit others, not ourselves. By doing so, we will actually be benefiting ourselves, since we are all parts of the soul of *Adam ha Rishon*. Whether we like it or not, harming others returns to us, just like a boomerang returns to its thrower, and just as forcefully.

Let's recap for a moment. A corrected *Kli* is a desire used with altruistic intentions. And conversely, a corrupted *Kli* is a desire used with egoistic intentions. By using a *Kli* altruistically, we use a desire in the same way the Creator operates, and thus equalize with Him, at least concerning that specific desire. This is how we study His Thought.

So the only problem is to change the intentions with which we use our desires. But for that to happen, we must see at least one other way of using our desires. We need an example of what other intentions look or feel like. That way, we will at least be able to decide whether we want it or not. When we see no other way of using our desires, we're trapped in the ones we already have. In that state, how can we find other intentions? Is this a trap or are we missing something?

Kabbalists explain that we are not missing anything. This is a trap, but it's not a deadlock. If we follow the path of our *Reshimot*, an example of another intention will appear by itself. Now let's see what *Reshimot* are, and how they help us out of the trap.

RESHIMOT—BACK TO THE FUTURE

Reshimot—roughly speaking—are records, recollections of past states. Each *Reshimo* (singular for *Reshimot*) that a soul experiences along its spiritual path is collected in a special "data bank."

When we want to climb up the spiritual ladder, these *Reshimot* comprise our trail. They resurface one by one, and we relive them. The faster we re-experience each *Reshimo*, the faster we exhaust it and move on to the next in line, which is always higher up the ladder.

We cannot change the order of the *Reshimot*. That has already been determined on our way down. But we can and should determine what we will do with each *Reshimo*. If we are passive and simply wait for them to pass, it will take a long time before we thoroughly experience them, and before that happens they can cause us great pain. This is why the passive approach is called "the path of pain."

On the other hand, we can take an active approach by trying to relate to each *Reshimo* as to "another day in school," trying to see what the Creator is trying to teach us. If we simply remember that this world is the result of spiritual occurrences, this will be enough to tremendously speed up the passing of the *Reshimot*. This active approach is called "the path of Light," because our efforts connect us to the Creator, to the Light, instead of to our present state, as with the passive attitude.

Actually, our efforts don't have to succeed; the effort itself is enough. By increasing our desires to be like the Creator (altruistic), we attach ourselves to higher, more spiritual states.

The process of spiritual progress is very similar to the way children learn; it is basically a process of imitation. By imitating grownups, even though they don't know what they are doing, children's constant mimicry creates within them the *desire* to learn.

Note: It's not what they know that promotes their growth; it's the simple fact that they *want to know*. The desire to know is enough to evoke in them the next *Reshimo*, the one in which they already know.

Let's look at it from another angle: Initially, the fact that they wanted to know was not because it was their own choice, but because the present *Reshimo* exhausted itself, making the next *Reshimo* in line "want" to make itself known. Therefore, for the child to discover it, the *Reshimo* had to evoke in the child a desire to know it.

This is exactly how the spiritual *Reshimot* work on us. We are not really learning anything new in this world or in the spiritual world; we are simply climbing back to the future.

If we want to be more giving, like the Creator, we should constantly examine ourselves and see if we fit the description that we consider spiritual (altruistic). This way, our desire to be more altruistic will help us develop a more accurate, detailed perception of ourselves compared to the Creator.

If we do not want to be egoistic, our desires will evoke the *Reshimot* that will show us what being more altruistic means. Every time we decide that we do not want to use this or that desire egoistically, the *Reshimo* of that state is considered to have completed its task, and moves on to make room for the next. This is the only correction we are required to make. Kabbalist Yehuda Ashlag phrases this principle in these words: "...by hating the evil [egoism] in earnest truth it is corrected."

And then he explains: "...if two people come to realize that each hates what one's friend hates, and loves what and whom one's friend loves, they come into perpetual bonding, as a stake that will never fall. Hence, since the Creator loves to bestow, the lower ones should also adapt to want only to bestow. The Creator also hates to be a receiver, as He is completely whole and needs nothing. Thus, man too must hate the matter of reception for oneself. It follows from all the above that one must hate the will to receive bitterly, for all the ruins in the world come only from the will to receive. Through the hatred one corrects it."

Thus, simply by wanting it we evoke *Reshimot* of more altruistic desires, which already exist within us from the time when we were connected in the soul of *Adam ha Rishon*. These *Reshimot* correct us and make us more like our Creator. Therefore, desire (the *Kli*) is both the engine of change, as we've said in Chapter One, and the means for correction. We need not suppress our desires, just learn how to work with them productively for ourselves and for everyone else.

IN A NUTSHELL

For correct perception, we need to limit ourselves by three boundaries:

1. There are four categories to Perception: a) Matter; b) Form in Matter; c) Abstract Form; and d) Essence. We perceive only the first two.

2. All my perception occurs within my soul. My soul is my world and the world outside of me is so abstract that I can't even say for sure if it exists or not.

3. What I perceive is mine alone; I cannot pass it to anyone else. I can tell others about my experience, but when they experience it, they will certainly experience it in their own way.

When I perceive something, I measure it and determine what it is according to the qualities of the measurement tools I have within. If my tools are flawed, so will be my measurement; hence, my picture of the world will be distorted and incomplete.

Presently, we are measuring the world with five senses. But we need six senses to measure it correctly. This is why we are unable to manage our world productively and joyfully for all.

Actually, the sixth sense is not a physical sense, but an intention. It relates to how we use our desires. If we use them with the intention to give instead of to receive, meaning if we use them altruistically instead of egoistically, we will perceive a whole new world. This is why the new intention is called "the sixth sense."

Placing the altruistic intention over our desires makes them similar to those of the Creator. This similarity is called "equivalence of form" with the Creator. Having it grants its owner the same perception and knowledge as that of the Creator. This is why only with the sixth sense (intention to bestow) is it possible to really know how to conduct ourselves in this world.

When a new desire comes along, it actually isn't new. It is a desire that has already been in us, whose memory has been recorded in the data bank of our souls—the *Reshimot*. The chain of *Reshimot* leads straight to the top of the ladder—the Thought of Creation—and the faster we climb it, the more quickly and pleasantly we will reach our destiny.

The *Reshimot* appear one by one, at a rate we determine through our desire to ascend in spirituality, which is where they originate. When we try to learn from and understand each *Reshimo*, it is exhausted more quickly and the state of understanding it (which already exists) appears. When we understand a *Reshimo*, the next *Reshimo* in line surfaces, until finally all the *Reshimot* have been realized and studied, and we have reached the end of our correction.

6

THE (NARROW) ROAD TO FREEDOM

It might come as a surprise to you, but you already know quite a bit about Kabbalah. Flip back and let's review. You know that Kabbalah started about 5,000 years ago in Mesopotamia (today's Iraq). It was discovered when people were searching for the purpose of their lives. Those people discovered that the reason we are all born is to receive the ultimate pleasure of becoming like the Creator. When they discovered it, they built study groups and began to spread the word.

Those first Kabbalists told us that all we're made of is a will to receive pleasure, which they separated into five levels—still, vegetative, animate, speaking, and spiritual. The will to receive is very important because it's the engine behind everything we do in this world. In other words, we're always trying to receive pleasure, and the more we have, the more we want. As a result, we always evolve and change.

Later, we learned that Creation was formed in a four-phase process, where the Root (synonymous to the Light and the Creator) created the will to receive; the will to receive wanted to give, then decided to receive as a way of giving, and finally wanted to receive once more. But this time it wanted to receive the knowledge of how to be the Creator, the *Giver*.

After the four phases, the will to receive was divided into five worlds and one soul, called *Adam ha Rishon*. *Adam ha Rishon* broke and materialized in our world. In other words, all of us are actually one soul, connected and dependent on each other just like cells in a body. But when the will to receive grew, we became more self-centered and stopped feeling that we were one. Instead, today we only feel ourselves, and even if we do relate to others it is done to receive pleasure through them.

This egoistic state is called "the broken soul of *Adam ha Rishon*," and it is our task, as parts of that soul, to correct it. Actually, we don't have to correct it, but we do have to be aware that we cannot feel real pleasure in our present state because of the law of the will to receive: "When I have what I want, I no longer want it." When we realize that, we will begin to look for a way out of the trap of this law, the egoism trap.

Looking for freedom from the ego leads to the emergence of the "point in the heart," the desire for spirituality. The "point in the heart" is like any desire; it is increased and decreased through the influence of the environment. So if we want to increase our desire for spirituality, we need to build an environment that promotes spirituality. This last (but most important) chapter in our book will talk about what needs to be done to have a spirituality-supportive environment on personal, social, and international levels.

THE DARK
BEFORE THE DAWN

The darkest time of night is right before the dawn. Similarly, the writers of *The Book of Zohar* said, almost 2,000 years ago, that humanity's darkest time will come right before its spiritual awakening. For centuries, beginning with the Ari, author of the *Tree of Life*, who lived in the 16th century, Kabbalists have been writing that the time *The Zohar* was referring to was the end of the 20th century. They called it "the last generation."

They did not mean that we would all perish in some apocalyptic, spectacular event. In Kabbalah, a generation represents a spiritual state. The last generation is the last and *highest* state that can be reached. And Kabbalists said that the time we are living in—the beginning of the 21st century—is when we would see the generation of the spiritual ascent.

But these Kabbalists also said that for this change to happen, we cannot continue to develop the way we've been evolving thus far. They said that today, a conscious, free choice is required if we want to grow.

As with any beginning or birth, the emergence of the last generation, the generation of free choice, is no easy process. Until recently, we have been evolving in our lower desires—still through speaking—leaving out the spiritual level. But now the spiritual *Reshimot* (spiritual genes, if you will) are surfacing in millions of people, and demand to be realized in real life.

When these *Reshimot* first appear in us, we still lack the appropriate method to deal with them. They are like a whole new technology that we must still learn to deal with. So while we are learning, we are trying to realize the new kind of *Reshimot* with our old ways of thought, because those ways helped us realize our lower level *Reshimot*. But those ways are inadequate for handling the new *Reshimot*, and therefore fail to do their task, leaving us empty and frustrated.

When these *Reshimot* surface in an individual, frustration arises, then depression, until he or she learns how to relate to these new desires. This usually happens by applying the wisdom of Kabbalah, which was originally designed to cope with spiritual *Reshimot*, as we've described in Chapter One.

If, however, one cannot find the solution, the individual might plunge into workaholism, addictions of all kinds, and other attempts to suppress the problem of the new desires, trying to avoid coping with an incurable ache.

On a personal level, such a state is very distressing but it doesn't pose a problem serious enough to destabilize the social structure. However, when spiritual *Reshimot* appear in many millions of people at approximately the same time, and particularly if it happens in many countries simultaneously, you have a global crisis on your hands. And a global crisis calls for a global solution.

Clearly, humanity today is in a global crisis. Depression is soaring to unprecedented rates in the United States, but the picture isn't much brighter in other developed countries. In 2001, the World Health Organization (WHO) reported that "depression is the leading cause of disability in the U.S. and worldwide."

Another major problem in modern society is the alarming abundance of drug abuse. It's not that drugs haven't always been in use, but in the past they were used primarily for medicine and for rituals, while today they are being used at a much earlier age, primarily to alleviate the emotional void that so many young people feel. And because depression is soaring, so is the use of drugs and drug-related crimes.

Another facet of the crisis is the family unit. The family institution used to be an icon of stability, warmth, and shelter, but not any more. According to the National Center for Health Statistics, for every two couples that marry, one divorces, and the figures are similar throughout the Western world.

Moreover, it is no longer a situation where couples have to go through a major crisis or personality clash to decide on a divorce. Today, even couples in their 50s and 60s can't find reasons to stay together once their kids have left home. Since their incomes are secured, they're not afraid of starting a new page at ages that only a few years back were considered unacceptable for such steps. We've even got a clever name for it: the "empty nest syndrome." But the bottom line is that people divorce because once their children have left home, there is nothing to keep the parents together, since there is simply no love between them.

And this is the real void: the absence of love. If we remember that we were all created egoists by a force that wants to give, we might have a fighting chance. At least then we will know where to start looking for a solution.

But the crisis is unique not only in its universality, but in its versatility, which makes it much more comprehensive and difficult to handle. The crisis is happening in just about every field of human engagement—personal, social, international, in science, medicine, and the climate. For example, until just a few years ago, "the weather" was a convenient haven when one had nothing to contribute about other topics. Today, however, we are all required to be climate savvy. Hot topics nowadays are climate change, global warming, rising sea levels, and the start of the new hurricane season.

"The Big Thaw" is what Geoffrey Lean of *The Independent* ironically called the state of the planet in an online article published November 20, 2005. Here's the title of Lean's article: "The Big Thaw: Global Disaster Will Follow If the Ice Cap on Greenland Melts." And the subtitle, "Now scientists say it is vanishing far faster than even they expected."

And weather is not the only disaster lurking on the horizon. The June 22, 2006 issue of Nature magazine, published a University of California study stating that the San Andreas Fault is now overdue for the "big one." According to Yuri Fialko of Scripps Institution of Oceanography at the University of California, "the fault is a significant seismic hazard and is primed for another big earthquake."

And of course, if we survive the storms, the earthquakes, and the rising seas, there is always a Bin Laden in the area to remind us that our lives can be made significantly briefer than we had planned.

And last but not least, there are health issues that require our attention: AIDS, avian flu, mad cow, and of course, the old standbys: cancer, cardiovascular diseases, and diabetes. There are many more we can mention here, but by now you've probably gotten the point. Even though some of these health problems aren't new, they are mentioned here because they are rapidly spreading around the globe.

Conclusion: An ancient Chinese proverb says that when you want to curse someone, say, "May you live in interesting times." Our time is indeed very interesting; but it is not a curse. It is as *The Book of Zohar* promised—the darkness before the dawn. Now, let's see if there's a solution.

A BRAVE NEW WORLD IN FOUR STEPS

It takes only four steps to change the world:

1. Acknowledge the crisis;
2. Discover why it exists;
3. Determine the best solution;
4. Design a plan to resolve the crisis.

Let's examine them one at a time.

1. Acknowledging the crisis.

There are several reasons why many of us are still unaware that there is a crisis. Governments and international corporations should have been the first to tackle the issue, but conflicting interests prevent them from cooperating to deal with the crisis effectively. In addition, most of us still don't feel that the problem is threatening us in any personal way, and therefore we suppress the urgent need to deal with it, before the going gets much tougher.

The biggest problem is that we have no memory of such a precarious state in the past. Because of that, we're unable to assess our situation correctly. That's not to say that catastrophes never happened before, but our time is unique in the sense that today it is happening on all fronts, instantaneously—in every aspect of human life, and around the globe.

2. Discovering why it exists.

A crisis occurs when there's a collision between two elements, and the superior element forces its rule on the inferior one. Human nature, or egoism, is discovering how opposite it is from Nature, or altruism. This is why so many people feel distressed, depressed, insecure and frustrated.

In short, the crisis isn't really happening on the outside. Even though it certainly seems to take up physical space, it is happening within us. The crisis is the titanic struggle between the good (altruism) and the evil (egoism). How sad it is that we have to play the bad guys in the real reality show. But don't lose hope—as in all shows, a happy end awaits.

3. Determining the best solution.

The more we recognize the underlying cause of the crisis, namely our egoism, the more we'll understand what needs to be changed in us and in our societies. By doing so, we will be able to de-escalate the crisis and bring society and ecology to a positive, constructive outcome. We will talk more about such changes as we explore the idea of freedom of choice.

4. Designing a plan to resolve the crisis.

Once we've completed the first three stages of the plan, we can draw it up in greater detail. But even the best plan cannot succeed without the active support of leading, internationally recognized organizations. Therefore, the plan must have a broad base of international support from scientists, thinkers, politicians, and the United Nations, as well as the media and social organizations.

Actually, because we grow from one level of desire to the next, everything that is happening now is happening for the first time on the spiritual level of desire. But if we remember that we are at this level, we can use the knowledge of those who have already connected with spirituality in the same way we use our current scientific knowledge.

Kabbalists, who have already made it to the spiritual worlds, the root of our world, see the *Reshimot* (spiritual root) causing this state, and can guide us out of the problems we are facing from its source in the spiritual world. This way we will resolve the crisis easily and quickly because we'll know why things happen and what needs to be done about them. Think of it this way: If you knew that there were people who could predict the results of tomorrow's lottery, wouldn't you like them at your side when you're placing your bets?

There is no magic here, only knowledge of the rules of the game in the spiritual world. Through the eyes of a Kabbalist, we're not in a crisis, we're just a little disoriented, and hence keep betting on the wrong numbers. When we find our direction, resolving the (nonexistent) crisis will be a piece of cake. And so will be winning the lottery. And the beauty about Kabbalistic knowledge is that it has no copyrights; it belongs to everyone.

KNOW YOUR LIMITS

An Old Prayer

Lord, grant me strength to change what I can
change, courage to accept what I cannot change, and
the wisdom to discern between them.

In our own eyes, we are unique and independently act-
ing individuals. This is a common trait for all people.
Just think of the centuries of battles humanity has been
through, only to finally obtain the limited personal freedom we have today.

But we are not the only ones who suffer when our
freedom is taken. There isn't a single creature that can
be captured without a struggle. It is an inherent, natural
trait to object to any form of subjugation. Nevertheless,
even if we understand that all creatures deserve to be free,
it doesn't guarantee that we understand what being free
really means or if, and how, it is connected to the process
of correcting humanity's egoism.

If we honestly ask ourselves about the meaning of
freedom, we're likely to discover that very little of our
present thoughts about it will still hold when we're fin-
ished asking. So before we can talk about freedom, we
must know what it really means to be free.

To see if we understand freedom, we must look
within ourselves to see if we are capable of even one free
and voluntary act. Because our will to receive constantly

grows, we are always urged to find better and more rewarding ways to live. But because we are locked in a rat race, we have no choice in this matter.

On the other hand, if our will to receive is the cause of all this trouble, maybe there's a way to control it. If we could do so, perhaps we could control the whole race. Otherwise, without this control, the game would appear to be lost before it's even been played.

But if we are the losers, then who's the winner? With whom (or what) are we competing? We go about our business as though events depend on our decisions. But do they really? Wouldn't it be better to give up trying to change our lives and just go with the flow?

On the one hand, we've just said that Nature objects to any subjugation. But on the other hand, Nature doesn't show us which, if any of our actions is free, and where we are lured by an invisible Puppet Master into thinking we are free.

Moreover, if Nature works according to a Master Plan, could these questions and uncertainties be part of the scheme? Perhaps there's an ulterior reason that makes us feel lost and confused. Maybe confusion and disillusionment are the Puppet Master's way of telling us, "Hey, take another look at where you're all going, because if you're looking for Me, you're looking in the wrong direction."

Few will deny that we are, indeed, disoriented. However, to determine our direction, we have to know where to start looking. This can save us years of futile efforts. The first thing we want to find is where we have free and independent choice, and where we don't. Once we realize this, we will know where we should concentrate our efforts.

THE REINS OF LIFE

The whole of Nature obeys only one law: "The Law of Pleasure and Pain." If the only substance in Creation is the will to receive pleasure, then only one rule of behavior is required: attraction to pleasure and rejection from pain.

We humans are no exception to the rule. We follow a preinstalled design that entirely dictates our every move: we want to receive the most, and work the least. And if possible, we want it all for free! Therefore, in everything we do, even when we are not aware of it, we always try to choose pleasure and avoid pain.

Even when it seems as if we're sacrificing ourselves, we're actually receiving more pleasure from the "sacrifice" than from any other option we can think of at that moment. And the reason we deceive ourselves into thinking we have altruistic motives is because deceiving ourselves is more fun than telling ourselves the truth. As Agnes Repplier once put it, "There are few nudities so objectionable as the naked truth."

In Chapter Three we said that Phase Two gives, even though it is actually motivated by the same will to receive as in Phase One. This is the root of every "altruistic" action we "bestow" upon each other.

We see how everything we do follows a "calculation of profitability." For example, I calculate the price of a commodity compared to the prospective benefit from getting it. If I think that the pleasure (or lack of pain) from having the commodity will be greater than the price I must pay, I will tell my "inner broker": "Buy! Buy! Buy!" turning the lights green across my mental Wall Street board.

We can change our priorities, adopt different values of good and bad, and even "train" ourselves to become fearless. Moreover, we can make a goal so important in our eyes that any hardship on the way to achieving it would become meaningless, intangible.

If, for example, I want the social status and good wages associated with being a famous physician, I will strain, sweat, and toil for years in medical school and live through several more years of sleep deprivation during internship, hoping it will eventually pay off in fame and fortune.

Sometimes the calculation of immediate pain for future gain is so natural, we don't even notice we're doing it. For example, if I became terribly ill and discovered that only a specific surgery could save my life, I would gladly have the operation. Because even though the operation itself might be very unpleasant and could pose risks of its own, it is not as threatening as my illness. In some cases I would even pay considerable sums to put myself through the ordeal.

CHANGING SOCIETY TO CHANGE MYSELF

Nature didn't only "sentence" us to a constant escape from suffering, and a continual pursuit of pleasure, it also denied us the ability to determine the kind of pleasure we want. In other words, we can't control what we want, and desires pop up within us without forewarning and without asking our opinion in the matter.

Yet, Nature not only created our desires, it also provided us with a way to control them. If we remember that we are all parts of the same soul, that of *Adam ha Rishon*, it will be easy for us to see that the way to control our own desires is by affecting the whole soul, meaning humanity, or at least a part of it.

Let's look at it this way: If a single cell wanted to go left, but the rest of the body wanted to go right, the cell would have to go right, too. That is, unless it convinced the whole body, or an overwhelming majority of the cells, or the body's "government," that it was better to go left.

So even though we can't control our own desires, society can and does control them. And because we can control our choice of society, we can choose the kind of society that will affect us in the way we think is best. Put simply, we can use social influences to control our own desires. And by controlling our desires, we'll control our thoughts and ultimately, our actions.

The Book of Zohar, almost two thousand years ago, had already described the importance of society. But since the 20th century, when it became obvious that we are dependent on each other for survival, effectively utilizing our societal dependency has become vital for spiritual progress. The paramount importance of society is a message that Kabbalist Yehuda Ashlag makes very clear in many of his essays, and if we follow his line of thought we will understand why.

Ashlag says that everyone's greatest wish, whether one admits it or not, is to be liked by others and to win their approval. It not only gives us a sense of confidence, but affirms our most precious possession—our ego. Without society's approval, we feel that our very existence is ignored, and no ego can tolerate denial. This is why people often go to extremes to win others' attention.

And because our greatest wish is to win society's approval, we are compelled to adapt to (and adopt) the laws of our environment. These laws determine not only our behavior, but design our attitude and approach to everything we do and think.

This situation makes us unable to choose anything—from the way we live, to our interests, to how we spend our free time, and even to the food we eat and the clothes we wear. Moreover, even when we choose to dress contrary to fashion or regardless of it, we are still (trying to be) indifferent to a *certain social code* that we have chosen to ignore. In other words, if the fashion we've chosen to ignore hadn't existed, we wouldn't have had to ignore it and would probably have chosen a different dress code. Ultimately, the only way to change ourselves is to change the social norms of our environment.

FOUR FACTORS

But if we are nothing more than products of our environment, and if there is no real freedom in what we do, in what we think, and in what we want, can we be held responsible for our actions? And if we are not responsible for them, who is?

To answer these questions we must first understand the four factors that comprise us, and how we can work with them to acquire freedom of choice. According to Kabbalah, we're all controlled by four factors:

1. The "bed," also called "first matter";
2. Unchanging attributes of the bed;
3. Attributes that change through external forces;
4. Changes in the external environment.

Let's see what each of them means to us.

1. The Bed, the First Matter

Our unchanging essence is called "the bed." I can be happy or sad, thoughtful, angry, alone or with others. In whatever mood and in whichever society, the basic *me* never changes.

To understand the four-phase concept, let's think of the budding and dying of plants. Consider a stalk of wheat. When a wheat seed decays, it loses its form entirely. But even though it has completely lost its form, only a new stalk of wheat will emerge from that seed, and nothing else. This is because the bed hasn't changed; the essence of the seed remains that of wheat.

2. Unchanging Attributes of the Bed

Just as the bed is unchanging and wheat always produces new wheat, the way wheat seeds develop is also unchanging. A single stalk may produce more than one stalk in the new life-cycle, and the quantity and quality of the new buds might change, but the bed itself, the essence of the previous shape of the wheat, will remain unchanged. Put simply, no other plant can grow from a wheat seed but wheat, and all wheat plants will always go through the same growth pattern from the moment they sprout to the moment they wither.

Similarly, all human children mature in the same sequence of growth. This is why we (more or less) know when a child should start developing certain skills, and when it can start eating certain foods. Without this fixed pattern, we wouldn't be able to chart the growth curve of human babies, or of anything else, for that matter.

3. Attributes that Change through External Forces

Even though the seed remains the same kind of seed, its appearance may change as a result of environmental influences such as sunlight, soil, fertilizers, moisture, and rain. So while the kind of plant remains wheat, its "wrapping," the attributes of the wheat's essence, can be modified through external elements.

Similarly, our moods change in the company of other people or in different situations even though our selves (beds) remain the same. Sometimes, when the influence of the environment is prolonged, it can change not only our mood, but even our character. It's not the environment that creates new traits in us; it's just that being among a certain kind of people encourages certain aspects of our nature to become more active than they were before.

4. Changes in the External Environment

The environment that affects the seed is in itself affected by other external factors such as climate changes, air quality, and nearby plants. This is why we grow plants in greenhouses and artificially fertilize the land. We try to create the best environment for plants to grow.

In our human society, we constantly change our environment: we advertise new products, elect governments, attend schools of all kinds, and spend time with friends. Therefore, to control our own growth, we should learn to control the kinds of people we spend time with, but most importantly, the people we look up to. Those are the people who will influence us most.

If we wish to become corrected—altruistic—we need to know what social changes will promote correction, and follow them through. With this last factor—the changes in the external environment—we shape our essence, change our bed's attributes, and consequently determine our fate. This is where we have freedom of choice.

CHOOSING
THE RIGHT ENVIRONMENT
FOR CORRECTION

Even though we cannot determine the attributes of our bed, we can still affect our lives and our destiny by choosing our social environments. In other words, because the environment affects the attributes of the bed, we can determine our own futures by building our environments in a way that promotes the goals we want to achieve.

Once I have chosen my direction and built an environment to steer me there, I can use society as a booster to accelerate my progress. If, for example, I want money, I can surround myself with people who want it, talk about it, and work hard to get it. This will inspire me to work hard for it as well, and turn my mind into a factory of money-making schemes.

And here's another example. If I am overweight and I want to change that, the easiest way to do it is to surround myself with people who think, talk, and encourage each other to lose weight. Actually, I can do more than surround myself with people to create an environment; I can reinforce the influence of that environment with books, films, and magazine articles. Any means that increases and supports my desire to lose weight will do.

It's all in the environment. AA, drug rehabilitation institutions, Weight Watchers, all of these use the power of society to help people when they cannot help themselves. If we use our environments correctly, we can achieve things we wouldn't dare to dream. And best of all, we wouldn't even feel as if we were making any effort to achieve them.

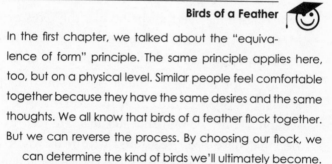

Birds of a Feather

In the first chapter, we talked about the "equivalence of form" principle. The same principle applies here, too, but on a physical level. Similar people feel comfortable together because they have the same desires and the same thoughts. We all know that birds of a feather flock together. But we can reverse the process. By choosing our flock, we can determine the kind of birds we'll ultimately become.

The desire for spirituality is no exception. If I want spirituality and I want to increase my desire for it, I need only have the right friends, books, and films around me. Human nature will do the rest. If a group of people decides to become like the Creator, nothing can stand in their way, not even the Creator Himself. Kabbalists call it, "My sons defeated Me."

So why aren't we seeing a spirituality rush? Well, there's a little hitch: *you can't feel spirituality until you already have it.* The problem is that without seeing or feeling the goal, it's very hard to really want it, and we already saw that it's very hard to get anything without a great desire for it.

Think of it this way: everything we want in our world is a result of some external influence on us. If I like pizza, it's because friends, parents, TV, something or someone told me about how good it is. If I want to be a lawyer, it's because society gave me the impression that being a lawyer somehow pays off.

But where in our society can I find something or someone to tell me that being like the Creator is great? Moreover, if no such desire exists in society, how did it suddenly appear in me? Did it pop up out of the blue?

No, not out of the blue; out of the *Reshimot*. It's a memory of the future. Let me explain. Way back, in Chapter Four, we said that *Reshimot* are records, memories that have been registered within us when we were higher up on the spirituality ladder. These *Reshimot* lie in our subconscious and emerge one by one, each evoking new or stronger desires from past states.

Moreover, because *all of us* were at one point higher up on the spiritual ladder, we will *all* feel the awakening of the desire to go back to those spiritual states when it is our time to experience them—the spiritual level of desires. This is why *Reshimot* are memories of our own future states.

Therefore, the question shouldn't be, "How come I have a desire for something the environment didn't introduce to me?" Instead, we should ask, "Once I have this desire, how do I make the most of it?" And the answer is simple: Treat it as you would treat anything else you want to achieve—think about it, talk about it, read about it, and sing about it. Do everything you can to make it important, and your progress will accelerate proportionally.

In The Mishnah (*Pirkey Avot* 6:10), there is an inspiring (and true) story of a wise man by the name of Rabbi Yosi Ben Kisma, the greatest Kabbalist of his time. One day, a rich merchant from another town approached him and offered to relocate the Rabbi to the rich man's town to open a seminary for the town's wisdom-thirsty people. The merchant explained that there were no sages in his town, and that the town was in need of spiritual teachers. Needless to say, he promised Rabbi Yosi that all his personal and educational needs would be generously cared for.

To the merchant's great surprise, Rabbi Yosi declined resolutely, stating that under no circumstances would he move to a place where there were no other sages. The dismayed merchant tried to argue and suggested that Rabbi Yosi was the greatest sage of the generation and that he didn't need to learn from anyone.

"In addition," said the merchant, "by moving to our town and teaching our people, you would be doing a great spiritual service, since here there is already a great number of sages, and our town hasn't any. This would be a significant contribution to the spirituality of the whole generation. Would the great Rabbi at least consider my offer?"

To that, Rabbi Yosi resolutely replied: "Even the wisest sage will soon become unwise when dwelling among unwise people." It is not that Rabbi Yosi didn't want to help the merchant's townsmen; he simply knew that without a supportive environment, he would lose doubly—failing to enlighten his students, and losing his own spiritual degree.

NO ANARCHISTS

The previous section may lead you to think that Kabbalists are anarchists who are willing to obstruct social order to promote building spirituality-oriented societies. Nothing could be further from the truth.

Yehuda Ashlag explains very clearly, and any sociologist and anthropologist will confirm, that human beings are social creatures. In other words, we don't have a choice but to live in societies because we are offshoots of one common soul. It is therefore clear that we must also conform to the rules of the society we live in and care for its wellbeing. And the only way to achieve that is if we adhere to the rules of the society we live in.

However, Ashlag also states that in any situation that is *not* related to society, society has no right or justification to limit or oppress the freedom of the individual. Ashlag even goes so far as to call those who do so "criminals," stating that concerning one's spiritual progress, Nature does not oblige the individual to obey the majority's will. On the contrary, spiritual growth is the personal responsibility of each and every one of us. By doing so, we are improving not only our own lives, but the lives of the whole world.

It is imperative that we understand the separation between our obligations to the society we live in and to our personal spiritual growth. Knowing where to draw the line and how to contribute to both will free us from much confusion and misconceptions about spirituality.

The rule in life should be simple and straightforward: In everyday life we obey the rule of law; in spiritual life we're free to evolve individually. It turns out that individual freedom can only be achieved through our choice in spiritual evolvement, where others must not interfere.

THE EGO'S INEVITABLE DEATH

The love of liberty is the love of others;
the love of power is the love of ourselves.

—William Hazlitt (1778 - 1830)

Let's take a moment for another look at the basics of Creation. The only thing that the Creator created is our will to receive, our egoism. This is our essence. If we learn how to "deactivate" our egoism, we will restore our connection with the Creator, because without selfishness, we will regain equivalence of form with Him, as it exists in the spiritual worlds. Deactivating our egoism is the beginning of our climb up the spiritual ladder, the beginning of the correction process.

It is Nature's ironic humor that people who indulge in selfish pleasures cannot be happy. There are two reasons for that: 1) As we explained in Chapter One, egoism is a Catch-22: if you have what you want, you no longer want it. And 2) A selfish desire enjoys not only the satisfaction of its own whims, but the dissatisfaction of others'.

To better understand the second reason, we need to go back to the basics. Phase One in the Four Basic Phases wants only to receive pleasure. Phase Two is already more sophisticated, and wants to receive pleasure from giving because giving is the Creator's state of being. If our development had stopped at Phase One, we would be satisfied the minute our desires were fulfilled and wouldn't care what others had.

However, Phase Two—the desire to give—compels us to notice others so we can give to them. But because our basic desire is to receive, all we see when we look at other people is that "they have all kinds of things that I don't." Because of Phase Two, we will always compare ourselves to others, and because of Phase One's will to receive, we always want to be above them. This is why we take pleasure in their deficiencies.

By the way, this is also why the poverty line changes from country to country. According to Webster's Dictionary, the poverty line is "a level of personal or family income below which one is classified as poor according to governmental standards."

If everyone around me were as poor as I am, I wouldn't feel poor. But if everyone around me were wealthy, and I only had an average income, I'd feel like the poorest person on Earth. In other words, our norms are dictated by the combination of Phase One (what we want to have) and Phase Two (which is determined by what others have).

In fact, our desire to give, which should have been the guarantee that our world would be a good place to live in, is actually the reason for all the evil in this world. This is the essence of our corruption, so replacing the intention to receive with an intention to give is all that we need to correct.

THE CURE

No desire or quality is naturally evil; it's how we use them that make them so. Ancient Kabbalists already said: "Envy, lust, and (the pursuit of) honor bring a man out of the world," meaning out of our world and into the spiritual world.

How so? We've already seen that envy leads to competitiveness, and competitiveness generates progress. But envy leads to far greater results than technological or other worldly benefits. In the *Introduction to The Book of Zohar*, Ashlag writes that humans can sense others, and therefore lack what others have. As a result, they are filled with envy and want everything that others have, and the more they have, the emptier they feel. In the end, they want to devour the whole world.

Eventually, envy brings us to settle for nothing less than the Creator Himself. But here Nature's humor plays a trick on us once more: The Creator is a desire to give, altruism. Although we are initially unaware of it, by wanting to take the driver seat and be Creators, we are actually craving to become altruists. Thus, through envy—the ego's most treacherous and harmful trait—our egoism puts itself to death, just as cancer destroys its host organism until it, too, dies with the body it has ruined.

Once again we can see the importance of building the right social environment, because if we are forced to be jealous, we should at least be *constructively* jealous, meaning jealous of something that will bring us to correction.

Kabbalists describe egoism like this: Egoism is like a man with a sword that has a drop of enchantingly luscious, but lethal potion at its tip. The man knows that the potion is a venomous poison, but cannot help himself. He opens his mouth, brings the tip of the sword to his tongue, and swallows...

A just and happy society cannot rely on monitored or "channeled" selfishness. We can try to restrain egoism through rule of law, but this will work just until circumstances toughen, as we've seen with Germany—a democracy until it democratically elected Adolf Hitler. We can also try to channel egoism to benefit society, but that has already been tried in Russia's communism, and failed miserably.

Even America, the land of freedom of opportunity and capitalism, is failing to make its citizens happy. According to the New England Journal of Medicine, "Annually, more than 46 million Americans, ages 15-54, suffer from depressive episodes." And the Archives of General Psychiatry announced: "The use of potent antipsychotic drugs to treat children and adolescents... increased more than fivefold between 1993 and 2002," as published on the June 6, 2006 edition of *The New York Times*.

In conclusion, as long as egoism has the upper hand, society will always be unjust and will disappoint its own members one way or another. Eventually, all egoism-based societies will exhaust themselves along with the egoism that created them. We just have to make it happen as quickly and as easily as we can, for everybody's benefit.

FAKE FREEDOM

Kabbalists relate to the absence of the sensation of the Creator as "concealment of the Creator's face." This concealment creates an illusion of freedom to choose between our world and the Creator's (spiritual) world. If we could see the Creator, if we could really sense the benefits of altruism, we would undoubtedly prefer His world to ours, as His world is a world of giving and of pleasure.

But because we do *not* see the Creator, we don't follow His rules, and instead, constantly break them. In fact, even if we did know the Creator's rules, but did not see the pain we inflict on ourselves by breaking them, we would most likely still break them because we would think that it's much more fun to remain egoists.

Earlier in this chapter, in the section, "The Reins of Life," we said that the whole of Nature obeys only one law: The Law of Pleasure and Pain. In other words, everything we do, think, and plan is designed to either diminish our pain or increase our pleasure. We have no freedom in that. But because we don't see that we are governed by these forces, we *think* we are free.

Concealment

Baruch Ashlag, Yehuda Ashlag's son and a great Kabbalist in his own right, wrote down in a notebook words he'd heard from his father. The notebook was later published under the title, *Shamati (I Heard)*. In one of his notes, he wrote that if we were created by an Upper Force, why is it that we don't feel it? Why is it hidden? If we knew what it wanted of us, we wouldn't be making mistakes and we wouldn't be tormented by punishment.

How simple and joyous would life have been if the Creator had been revealed! We wouldn't doubt His existence and we could all recognize His guidance over us and over the whole world. We would know the reason and the purpose of our creation, see His reactions to our actions, communicate with Him and ask His counsel before every act. How beautiful and simple life would be!

Ashlag ends his thoughts with the inevitable conclusion: Our one aspiration in life should be to reveal the Creator.

However, to really be free, we must first be freed from the reins of the pleasure-and-pain law. And because our egos dictate what is pleasurable and what is painful, we find that to be free, we must first be liberated from our egos.

CONDITIONS FOR FREE CHOICE

Ironically, true freedom of choice is possible only if the Creator is concealed. This is because if one option seems preferable, our egoism leaves us no choice but to go for it. In that case, even if we choose to give, it will be giving in order to receive, or egoistic giving. For an act to be truly altruistic and spiritual, its benefits must be hidden from us.

If we keep in mind that the whole purpose of Creation is to eventually be liberated from egoism, our actions will always be heading in the right direction—towards the Creator. Therefore, if we have two choices and we don't know which of them would bring more pleasure (or less pain), then we have a real opportunity to make a free choice.

If the ego does not see a preferable choice, we can choose according to a different set of values. For example, we could ask ourselves not what would be more fun, but what would be more giving. If giving is something we value, this will be easy to do.

We can either be egoists or altruists, either think of ourselves or think of others. There are no other options. Freedom of choice is possible when both options are clearly visible and equally appealing (or unappealing). If I can only see one option, I will have to follow it. Therefore, to choose freely, I have to see my own nature and the Creator's nature. Only if I don't know which is more pleasurable can I make a truly free choice and neutralize my ego.

IMPLEMENTING FREE CHOICE

The first principle in spiritual work is "faith above reason." So before we talk about implementing free choice, we must explain the Kabbalistic meanings of "faith" and "reason."

FAITH

In just about every religion and belief system on Earth, faith is used as a means to compensate for what we cannot see or clearly perceive. In other words, because we cannot see God, we have to *believe* that He exists. In this case, we use faith to compensate for our inability to see God. This is called "blind faith."

But faith is used as compensation not just in religion, but in practically everything we do. How do we know, for example, that the Earth is round? Did we ever fly to outer space to check it out for ourselves? We believe the scientists who tell us that it's round because we think of scientists as reliable people that we can trust when they say they checked it out. We believe them; it's faith. Blind faith.

So wherever and whenever we cannot see for ourselves, we use faith to complete the missing pieces of the picture. But this is not solid information—it is just blind faith.

In Kabbalah, faith means the exact opposite of what we just described. Faith, in Kabbalah, is a tangible, vivid, complete, unbreakable, and irrefutable perception of the Creator—of life's rule of law. Therefore, the only way to acquire faith in the Creator is to become exactly like Him. Otherwise, how will we know beyond a shadow of a doubt exactly who He is, or that He even exists?

REASON

Webster's Dictionary offers two definitions for the term, "reason." The first definition is "cause," but it's the second definition that interests us. Reason, according to Webster's, has three meanings:

1. The power of comprehending, inferring or thinking, especially in orderly rational ways.
2. Proper exercise of the mind.
3. The sum of the intellectual powers.

As synonyms, Webster's offers these options (among others): intelligence, mind, and logic.

Now let's read some of the insightful words Kabbalist Baruch Ashlag wrote in a letter to a student, explaining Creation's "chain of command." This will clarify why we need to go *above* reason.

"The will to receive was created because the purpose of Creation was to do good to His creatures, and for this purpose there must be a vessel to receive pleasure. After all, it is impossible to feel pleasure if there is no need for the pleasure, because without a need, no pleasure is felt.

"This will to receive is all the man (Adam) that the Creator created. When we say that man will be imparted eternal delight, we refer to the will to receive, which will receive all the pleasure that the Creator planned to give it.

"The will to receive has been given servants to serve it. Through them, we will receive pleasure. These servants are the hands, the legs, the sight, the hearing, etc. All of them are considered one's servants. In other words, the will to receive is the master and the organs are its servants.

"And as it usually happens, the servants have a butler among them who watches over the master's servants, ensuring that they work for the desired purpose of bringing pleasure, as this is what the master—the will to receive—wants.

"And if one of the servants is absent, the pleasure related to that servant will be absent, too. For example, if one is deaf, he or she will not be able to enjoy music. And if one cannot smell, one will not be able to enjoy the fragrance of perfume.

"But if one's brain is missing (the supervisor of the servants), which is like the foreman who watches over the workers, the whole business will collapse and the owner will suffer losses. If one has a business with many employees but lacks a good manager, one might lose instead of profit.

"However, even without the manager (reason), the boss (the will to receive) is still present. And even if the manager dies, the boss still lives. The two are unrelated."

It turns out that if we want to beat the will to receive and become altruists, we must first overcome its "chief of staff"—our very own reason. Therefore, "faith above reason" means that faith—becoming exactly like the Creator—should be above (more important than) reason—our egoism.

And the way to come by that is twofold: On the personal level, it is a study group and a circle of friends that will help create a social environment promoting spiritual values. And on the collective level, it requires that the whole society learns to appreciate altruistic values.

IN A NUTSHELL

Everything we do in life is determined by the pleasure and pain principle: we run from pain and chase pleasure. And the less we have to work for the pleasure, the better.

The pleasure and pain principle is dictated by the will to receive, and the will to receive controls everything we do, because that's our essence. Therefore, while we think we are free beings, we are actually chained by the two reins of life, pleasure and pain, held in the hands of our egoism.

Four factors determine who we are: 1) the Bed, 2) the unchanging attributes of the Bed, 3) attributes that change through external forces, and 4) changes in the external environment. We can influence only the last factor, but that factor influences all other factors.

Therefore, the only way to choose who we are is by choosing the last factor, thus monitoring and changing our social external environment. Because changes in the last factor affect all other factors, by changing it we will change ourselves. If we want to liberate ourselves from egoism, we need to change the external environment to one that supports altruism, not egoism.

And once we've been liberated from the will to receive, from the shackles of egoism, we can advance in spirituality. To do that, we follow the principle of "faith above reason."

"Faith," in Kabbalah, means complete perception of the Creator. We can acquire faith by becoming equal to Him in our attributes, in our desires, intentions, and thoughts. The term "reason" relates to our mind, the "foreman" of our egoism. To go above it, we must make the value of equivalence with the Creator more important, more precious to us than any egoistic pleasure we can imagine.

On the personal level, we increase the importance of the Creator (altruism) by using books (or other forms of media), friends, and a teacher who show us how important it is to be altruistic. On the social level, we try to embrace more altruistic values in society.

However, and this is imperative to the success of the change, embracing altruistic values should *not* be done merely to make our lives more pleasant in this world. It *should* be done to equalize our selves and our societies with Nature, meaning with the only law of reality—the law of altruism—the Creator.

When we surround ourselves with these environments, as individuals and as a society, our values will gradually change to the values of our environment, thus transforming our egoism into altruism naturally, easily, and pleasantly.

FURTHER READING

Kabbalah for Beginners: *Kabbalah for Beginners* is a book for all those seeking answers to life's essential questions. We all want to know why we are here, why there is pain, and how we can make life more enjoyable. The four parts of this book provide us with reliable answers to these questions, as well as clear explanations of the gist of Kabbalah and its practical implementations.

Part One discusses the discovery of the wisdom of Kabbalah, and how it was developed, and finally concealed until our time. Part Two introduces the gist of the wisdom of Kabbalah, using ten easy drawings to help us understand the structure of the spiritual worlds, and how they relate to our world. Part Three reveals Kabbalistic concepts that are largely unknown to the public, and Part Four elaborates on practical means you and I can take, to make our lives better and more enjoyable for us and for our children.

Awakening to Kabbalah: a distinctive, personal, and awe-filled introduction to an ancient wisdom tradition. Rav Laitman—a disciple of the great Kabbalist Rabbi Baruch Ashlag (son of Yehuda Ashlag)—provides you with a deeper understanding of the fundamental teachings of Kabbalah, and how you can use this wisdom to clarify your relationship with others and the world around you.

Using language both scientific and poetic, he probes the most profound questions of spirituality and existence. This provocative, unique guide will inspire and invigorate you to see beyond the world as it is and the limitations of your everyday life, become closer to the Creator, and reach new depths of the soul.

Wondrous Wisdom: This book offers an initial course on Kabbalah. Like all the books presented here, *Wondrous Wisdom* is based solely on authentic teachings passed down from Kabbalist teacher to student over thousands of years. At the heart of the book is a sequence of lessons revealing the nature of Kabbalah's wisdom and explaining how to attain it. For every person questioning "Who am I really?" and "Why am I on this planet?" this book is a must.

Kabbalah, Science, and the Meaning of Life: Science explains life's mechanisms; Kabbalah explains life's purpose. In *Kabbalah, Science, and the Meaning of Life*, Rav Michael Laitman, PhD, eloquently introduces earthshaking concepts so even readers unfamiliar with Kabbalah or science can easily understand.

Kabbalah explains that we are all one soul, materialized in many bodies. Similarly, modern science states that at the most fundamental level, we are all literally one. Science proves that reality is affected by its observer. Kabbalah states that reality, and even the Creator exist only within the observer. If you're just a little curious about reality and life's meaning, this is your book.

From Chaos to Harmony: Many researchers and scientists agree that the ego is the reason behind the perilous state our world is in today. Laitman's groundbreaking book not only demonstrates that egoism has been the basis for all suffering throughout human history, but also shows how we can turn our plight to pleasure.

The book contains a clear analysis of the human soul and its problems, and provides a "roadmap" of what we need to do to once again be happy. *From Chaos to Harmony* explains how we can rise to a new level of existence on personal, social, national, and international levels.

The Kabbalah Experience: The depth of the wisdom revealed in the questions and answers within this book will inspire readers to reflect and contemplate. This is not a book to race through, but rather one that should be read thoughtfully and carefully. With this approach, readers will begin to experience a growing sense of enlightenment while simply absorbing the answers to the questions every Kabbalah student asks along the way.

The Kabbalah Experience is a guide from the past to the future, revealing situations that all students of Kabbalah will experience at some point along their journeys. For those who cherish every moment in life, this book offers unparalleled insights into the timeless wisdom of Kabbalah.

The Path of Kabbalah: This unique book combines beginners' material with more advanced concepts and teachings. If you have read a book or two of Laitman's, you will find this book very easy to relate to.

While touching upon basic concepts such as perception of reality and Freedom of Choice, *The Path of Kabbalah* goes deeper and expands beyond the scope of beginners' books. The structure of the worlds, for example, is explained in greater detail here than in the "pure" beginners' books. Also described is the spiritual root of mundane matters such as the Hebrew calendar and the holidays.

The Science of Kabbalah: is the first in a series of texts that Rav Michael Laitman, Kabbalist and scientist, designed to introduce readers to the special language and terminology of the Kabbalah. Here, Rav Laitman reveals authentic Kabbalah in a manner that is both rational and mature. Readers are gradually led to an understanding of the logical design of the Universe and the life whose home it is.

The Science of Kabbalah, a revolutionary work that is unmatched in its clarity, depth, and appeal to the intellect, and will enable readers to approach the more technical works of Baal HaSulam (Rav Yehuda Ashlag), such as *Talmud Eser Sefirot* and *The Book of Zohar*. Although scientists and philosophers will delight in its illumination, laymen will also enjoy the satisfying answers to the riddles of life that only authentic Kabbalah provides. Now, travel through the pages and prepare for an astonishing journey into the Upper Worlds.

Introduction to the Book of Zohar: This volume, along with *The Science of Kabbalah*, is a required preparation for those who wish to understand the hidden message of *The Book of Zohar*. Among the many helpful topics dealt with in this text is an introduction to the "language of roots and branches," without which the stories in *The Zohar* are mere fable and legend. *Introduction to the Book of Zohar* will provide readers with the necessary tools to understand authentic Kabbalah as it was originally meant to be, as a means to attain the Upper Worlds.

The Zohar: annotations to the Ashlag commentary:

The Book of Zohar (*The Book of Radiance*) is an ageless source of wisdom and the basis for all Kabbalistic literature. Since its appearance nearly 2,000 years ago, it has been the primary, and often only, source used by Kabbalists.

For centuries, Kabbalah was hidden from the public, which was deemed not yet ready to receive it. However, our generation has been designated by Kabbalists as the first generation that is ready to grasp the concepts in The Zohar. Now we can put these principles into practice in our lives.

Written in a unique and metaphorical language, *The Book of Zohar* enriches our understanding of reality and widens our worldview. Although the text deals with one subject only—how to relate to the Creator—it approaches it from different angles. This allows each of us to find the particular phrase or word that will carry us into the depths of this profound and timeless wisdom.

Basic Concepts in Kabbalah: By reading within this book, one develops internal observations and approaches that did not previously exist within. This book is intended for contemplation of spiritual terms. To the extent that we are integrated with these terms, we begin to unveil the spiritual structure that surrounds us, almost as if a mist had been lifted.

Attaining the Worlds Beyond is a first step toward discovering the ultimate fulfillment of spiritual ascent in our lifetime. This book reaches out to all those who are searching for answers, who are seeking a logical and reliable way to understand the world's phenomena. This magnificent introduction to the wisdom of Kabbalah provides a new kind of awareness that enlightens the mind, invigorates the heart, and moves the readers to the depths of their soul.

Together Forever: On the surface, Together Forever is a children's story. But like all good children's stories, it transcends boundaries of age, culture, and upbringing.

In Together Forever, the author tells us that if we are patient and endure the trials we encounter along our life's path, we will become stronger, braver, and wiser. Instead of growing weaker, we will learn to create our own magic and our own wonders as only a magician can.

In this warm, tender tale, Michael Laitman shares with children and parents alike some of the gems and charms of the spiritual world. The wisdom of Kabbalah is filled with spellbinding stories. *The Magician* is yet another gift from this ageless source of wisdom, whose lessons make our lives richer, easier, and far more fulfilling.

Shamati: Rav Michael Laitman's words on the book: Among all the texts and notes that were used by my teacher, Rav Baruch Shalom Halevi Ashlag (the Rabash), there was one special notebook he always carried. This notebook contained the transcripts of his conversations with his father, Rav Yehuda Leib Halevi Ashlag (Baal HaSulam), author of the *Sulam* (Ladder) commentary on *The Book of Zohar*, *The Study of the Ten Sefirot* (a commentary on the texts of the Kabbalist, Ari), and of many other works on Kabbalah.

Not feeling well on the Jewish New Year's Eve of September 1991, the Rabash summoned me to his bedside and handed me a notebook, whose cover contained only one word, *Shamati* (I Heard). As he handed the notebook, he said, "Take it and learn from it." The following morning, my teacher perished in my arms, leaving me and many of his other disciples without guidance in this world.

Committed to Rabash's legacy to disseminate the wisdom of Kabbalah, I published the notebook just as it was written, thus retaining the text's transforming powers. Among all the books of Kabbalah, *Shamati* is a unique and compelling creation.

Kabbalah for the Student: *Kabbalah for the Student* offers authentic texts by Rav Yehuda Ashlag, author of the *Sulam* (Ladder) commentary on *The Book of Zohar*, his son and successor, Rav Baruch Ashlag, as well as other great Kabbalists. It also offers illustrations that accurately depict the evolution of the Upper Worlds as Kabbalists experience them. The book also contains several explanatory essays that help us understand the texts within.

In *Kabbalah for the Student*, Rav Michael Laitman, PhD, Rav Baruch Ashlag's personal assistant and prime student, compiled all the texts a Kabbalah student would need in order to attain the spiritual worlds. In his daily lessons, Rav Laitman bases his teaching on these inspiring texts, thus helping novices and veterans alike to better understand the spiritual path we undertake on our fascinating journey to the Higher Realms.

About Bnei Baruch

Bnei Baruch is a non-profit organization that is spreading the wisdom of Kabbalah to accelerate the spirituality of humankind. Kabbalist Rav Michael Laitman, PhD, who was the disciple and personal assistant to Rabbi Baruch Ashlag, the son of Rabbi Yehuda Ashlag (author of The Sulam commentary on *The Zohar*), follows in the footsteps of his mentor in leading the group toward its mission.

Laitman's scientific method provides individuals of all faiths, religions, and cultures with the precise tools necessary for embarking on a captivating path of self-discovery and spiritual ascent. With the focus being primarily on inner processes that individuals undergo at their own pace, Bnei Baruch welcomes people of all ages and lifestyles to engage in this rewarding process.

In recent years, a massive worldwide search for the answers to life's questions has been underway. Society has lost its ability to see reality for what it is and in its place superficial and often misleading concepts have appeared. Bnei Baruch reaches out to all those who are seeking awareness beyond the standard, people who are seeking to understand our true purpose for being here.

Bnei Baruch offers practical guidance and a reliable method for understanding the world's phenomena. The authentic teaching method, devised by Rabbi Yehuda Ashlag, not only helps overcome the trials and tribulations of everyday life, but initiates a process in which individuals extend themselves beyond their present boundaries and limitations.

Rabbi Yehuda Ashlag left a study method for this generation, which essentially "trains" individuals to behave as if they have already achieved the perfection of the Upper Worlds while still here in our world. In the words of Rabbi Yehuda Ashlag, "This method is a practical way to attain the Upper World, the source of our existence, while still living in this world."

A Kabbalist is a researcher who studies his or her own nature using this proven, time-tested and accurate method. Through this method, one attains perfection and control over one's life, and realizes life's true goal. Just as a person cannot function properly in this world without having knowledge of it, the soul cannot function properly in the Upper World without knowledge of it. The wisdom of Kabbalah provides this knowledge.

HOW TO CONTACT BNEI BARUCH

1057 Steeles Avenue West, Suite 532
Toronto, ON, M2R 3X1
Canada

Bnei Baruch USA,
2009 85th street, #51,
Brooklyn, NY 11214,
USA

E-mail: info@kabbalah.info
Web site: www.kabbalah.info

Toll free in USA and Canada:
1-866-LAITMAN
Fax: 1-905 886 9697